50 Creators of Children's Books

MEET
CANADIAN
AUTHORS
AND
ILLUSTRATORS

MEET CANADIAN AUTHORS AND ILLUSTRATORS

ALLISON GERTRIDGE

Scholastic Canada Ltd.

Scholastic Canada Ltd.
123 Newkirk Road, Richmond Hill, Ontario, Canada L4C 3G5

Scholastic Inc.
555 Broadway, New York, NY, 10012 USA

Ashton Scholastic Limited
Private Bag 92801, Penrose, Auckland, New Zealand

Ashton Scholastic Pty Limited
PO Box 579, Gosford, NSW 2250, Australia

Scholastic Publications Ltd
Villiers House, Clarendon Avenue, Leamington Spa,
Warwickshire, CV32 5PR UK

Canadian Cataloguing in Publication Data

Gertridge, Allison
Meet Canadian authors and illustrators

Includes bibliographic references.
ISBN 0-590-24319-5

1. Authors, Canadian - 20th century - Biography.
2. Illustrators - Canadian - Biography.
3. Children's literature, Canadian - Bio-bibliography.
4. Illustrated books, Children's - Canada -
Bio-bibliography. I. Title.

PS8081.G47 1994   C810.9'9282   C94-931126-X
PR9186.2.G47 1994

Design and desktop publishing by Think Publishing.

7 6 5 4 3 2 1   Printed in Canada   4 5 6 7 8/9

Contents

Continued

Introduction

"Read everything you can get your hands on," insist authors and illustrators from across the country. "Read and you will become a better writer *and* a better artist!"

And so, *my* opening words of advice are that you make it your goal to read all of the terrific titles listed on the following pages. And when you've finished, pass each and every fantastic one along to your students.

The authors and illustrators in this book are regular people. They have good days when ideas come by the dozens, and bad days when they don't come at all. And they all recall a time when getting published seemed almost impossible. They found their success not by magic, but through the encouragement of friends, family and teachers, and in the inspiring words and drawings of the authors and illustrators who came before them.

Sharing good books with your students is the single best way of helping them to become better readers, writers and artists. And who knows, maybe one day in the not-so-distant future one of your students will gaze down at the pages of her first published book and recall how important *your* encouragement was in the early years.

Warabé Aska

SELECTED TITLES

Who Goes to the Park
1984

Who Hides in the Park
1986

 Seasons
1990

 Aska's Animals
1991

 Aska's Birds
1992

 Aska's Sea Creatures
1994

 Illustrations only.

Born:
February 3, 1944, in Kagawa, Japan

Home:
Mississauga, Ontario

Warabé Aska was raised by his grandmother in the Japanese countryside. As a boy, he never had the opportunity to read books, as he couldn't afford to buy any and there was no library. There were, however, plenty of other things to do. Warabé remembers catching fish in the river and climbing fruit trees, the sorts of activities that appear in the pictures of all of his books today. "Living in the countryside influenced me greatly," says Warabé. "My contact with nature during this period has remained with me as a great influence on my work."

In fact, Warabé believes so strongly in the environment that continues to inspire him that he's currently one of a dozen artists working with a group called Artists for the Earth Renewal. "It's a grow-ing network of leading Canadian artists who have a special interest in environmental issues."

Warabé Aska attended art school, where he studied commercial art, but he didn't find much encouragement there. "The art teacher didn't regard my artistic efforts too highly, so I entered my oil paintings in all sorts of competitions to give me confidence, and interestingly I won awards in most of the contests I entered."

Thus encouraged, Warabé finished school and found work as a graphic designer. But he soon decided that what he really wanted to do was paint. "When I turned thirty, I quit that job and travelled around Japan for three months. While travelling, I made lots of sketches and paintings, and after that I had my first one-man show in Tokyo. At that time, many editors and publishers for adults and children came into the gallery and were interested in my art. Then several publishers commissioned me and I started work as an illustrator."

Warabé works on a number of paintings simultaneously because the oil paints he uses need time to dry. He works between eight and ten hours a day, from sun-up to sun-down, because he says daylight is important when you're trying to convey colours and light.

THE REAL THING

One of Warabé's first Canadian books was *Aska's Animals.* For this book, Warabé spent one whole month in the library, where he selected the most popular animals from around the world and learned all about their behaviour. But his research didn't end there. "I took part in a three-week safari in Kenya, observing and sketching the real animals and their surroundings. Zoo animals don't inspire anything in me because they are lazy; I must observe the real thing."

Warabé doesn't always travel great distances to do his sketches, though. "I always get something while I'm out walking, travelling or driving rather than staying at my studio. Getting out in the open air inspires me. Natural objects like trees, flowers, birds, animals, the sun and moon, clouds and the water trigger my imagination, and my observation of these objects gives me ideas."

So where, one might ask, did he get the idea to make the figures in his paintings fly? Warabé explains that this idea came from a lifelong wish to be able to fly himself. "If I were a bird or an airplane I would fly everywhere in the world. The sky is a huge canvas for me, and even now I am expressing my desire in my paintings."

Warabé says that his favourite part of being an illustrator is being able to communicate with large audiences through his books.

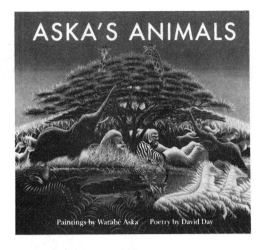

ASKA'S ANIMALS

Paintings by Warabé Aska   Poetry by David Day

"When I was working for the galleries I could communicate only with the collectors; my artwork would hang in their living rooms where many people could not see it."

Books, of course, reach all kinds of people in all kinds of places. Through them, Warabé hopes to encourage his readers to get outside and look at the wonders of nature.

In fact, Warabé was recently delighted to learn that he had reached what must be his youngest fan yet, when he received a letter from a mother in Calgary who wrote that her fourteen-month-old daughter prefers *Who Hides in the Park* to all of the other books in her collection. "I hadn't thought such a tiny tot could understand such a detailed style, but this little girl understood my art!" says Warabé. "That letter was a great encouragement to me!"

"Don't copy anyone else. Draw what you see and develop your own style. Originality is the most important thing."

SEASONS

WARABÉ ASKA *with poetry selected by Alberto Manguel*

DO IT YOURSELF!

Even when his art teacher discouraged him, Warabé Aska sought encouragement from other people. If you're serious about becoming an illustrator, you might want to try what Warabé Aska did and enter your work in a contest.

Michael Bedard

SELECTED TITLES

A Darker Magic
1987

The Lightning Bolt
1989

Redwork
*(CLA Book of the Year Award
for Children, Governor
General's Literary Award,
IODE Violet Downey Book
Award)*
1990

The Tinder Box
1990

The Nightingale
1991

Emily
1992

Painted Devil
1994

Born:
June 26, 1949, in Toronto,
Ontario

Home:
Toronto, Ontario

Michael Bedard didn't do a lot of reading when he was a boy; he confesses that the most involved he became with his copy of *Tom Sawyer* was the time he spent on a sunny afternoon burning a hole in its cover with a magnifying glass.

It wasn't until Michael was seventeen that he was bitten by the writing bug. His introduction to the craft was through poetry. "I had a teacher that year who was mad keen about poetry. Being in the presence of someone who was himself really in love with the shapes and sounds of words caught me just at the right point. During the course of that year I discovered a number of people, like T.S. Eliot, [Emily] Dickinson and William Blake. I began writing, and it didn't take too long before I began to fall in love with what I call the taste of words on the tongue, and by the end of that year I was writing poetry."

In fact, Michael became so serious about poetry that he skipped his grade twelve math exam in order to spend time at the local library reading Dylan Thomas!

After writing poetry for a number of years, Michael switched to novels. He received a number of rejections for his first effort, and so decided to put that premier novel aside and began working on his second, *A Darker Magic*. "Often the first book — a big book like that — is sort of a seed book. You dig down and you get all of these things out. I've gone back and I've used bits and pieces of that book in things that I've done afterwards, but the book itself will probably never see the light."

Michael uses a lot of reference material to direct his writing; his collections have become so extensive that he needs two rooms to accommodate them all. "When I begin to work on a piece, I build a wall above my desk — and it's a wall of pictures that relate to the piece I'm working on. For instance, when I started work on *Redwork*, I put up various pictures of people in magazines who might have reminded me something of the characters I was working on, pictures of various alchemical things I might have come across. I find that with each book that I work on, I tend to put pictures up on the wall to sort of lead me into the book."

THE HAND-HEART CONNECTION

Michael prefers to work in a room with a door that he can close, and he always writes with a pencil in notebooks. He describes what he calls the hand-heart connection that he experiences when writing a first draft in longhand. "I think your personality comes across in the actual writing if you write with a pencil, much more than if you were to go directly to type. When words come out in type you tend to be seduced by the look of the type; things look much more finished than they are. The tendency is to be satisfied with less than your best work."

Emily
by Michael Bedard · pictures by Barbara Cooney

What does Michael strive to achieve in *his* best work? "When I work on a piece, I'm careful not to say everything. Less is better when I'm writing. If I can leave things out, then I do, because I think it's very important to leave spaces for the reader to participate by fleshing it out with his or her own imagination. The book is not complete until the reader comes to it; it's not something that you stand back and look at, like a piece of art; it's something that you enter into and complete."

"I think a large part of what makes one a writer is not just dealing with the good times when words are coming, but being able to persist through the times when nothing is coming."

"It's important that readers realize that a book is not like watching television where it's all done for you. What *you* bring to it is vitally important.

"I think it was Joseph Campbell who said that you should follow your bliss, and I believe that's true. For me, writing is my bliss, and the favourite part of it is following that bliss and seeing where it will lead me. There's a profound joy for me in creating something beyond myself."

DO IT YOURSELF!

Michael Bedard often reflects on the images he brings to the books he reads. Try it yourself. Read something, then close the book and think about what you've read. Picture it in your mind. Then go back to the book and look for differences between the words you have read and the images in your head. What have you added to the passage from your own imagination that wasn't described on the page?

Eric Beddows

SELECTED TITLES

Zoom at Sea
(Amelia Frances Howard-Gibbon Illustrator's Award)
1983

Zoom Away
(Amelia Frances Howard-Gibbon Illustrator's Award)
1985

The Emperor's Panda
1986

Night Cars
(Elizabeth Mrazik-Cleaver Canadian Picture Book Award)
1988

Joyful Noise
1989

Shadow Play
1990

Who Shrank My Grandmother's House?
1992

Zoom Upstream
1992

The Rooster's Gift
1994

Born:
November 29, 1951, in Woodstock, Ontario

Home:
Stratford, Ontario

When he was in school, Eric Beddows was an ambitious reader. "The biggest book in the school library was Darwin's *Voyage of the Beagle* — 'big' in the sense of being the thickest book — so I decided to read that, because I thought everyone would be quite impressed. I don't think anyone *was* quite impressed, but it got me really interested in science and evolution which is still one of my main interests."

Eric was more particular about choosing his illustrators, however. "In my school books, I actually kept lists of illustrators I liked and didn't like — like baseball cards or sports heroes — only mine were Walter Crane and Rockwell Kent. But I didn't really think about becoming an illustrator myself until Tim Wynne-Jones asked me to illustrate *Zoom at Sea*."

Those illustrations, like his other work, have a very special appeal for Eric's young fans. Kids often ask him how he makes his pictures look so real. He tells them, "As a child, I didn't like it when an illustrator glossed over things or didn't bother to fill something in. My desire was always to make a picture feel like you could walk into it, and the way to do that is to know everything about the day that you're drawing. Is it sunny? Is it chilly? Is the wind blowing? Know all the little things, even though they seem like they're not important to the story, because we're always in weather and we're always in light or darkness."

To achieve this desired realism, Eric has run and participated in life drawing classes every week for the last fifteen years. He also does a lot of picture research and keeps clippings in an idea file for quick reference. So, although Zoom in the Zoom books was based on author Tim Wynne-Jones's cat, Montezooma, the cat you see in the books was actually modelled after a picture of a cat from Eric's idea file.

TOO MANY IDEAS

Eric rarely runs out of ideas. In fact, he's more often faced with the problem of having too many. He recalls reading a favourite artist's description of a nightmare in which before his eyes he saw all of the pictures he wasn't going to have time to paint, and insists that he has the same dream all the time.

To decide which ideas to discard, Eric does some careful thinking. "To get back on track, I have to get back to the basics of what I'm trying to say with this book. You can't do all things."

Eric's favourite part of illustrating a book comes after he's made those first decisions and is already into a job. "The illustrations pass a point where they take on a life of their own. It always reminds me of pushing a big rock up a hill. It's really hard to do until it gets to the top, and then it starts to roll down and it's really easy and really fun and a lot happens."

Eric's advice for young artists is: "Keep drawing if you like drawing. A person doesn't sit down and make one drawing from beginning to end. It's a process. It's something that you do over and over. So, if you enjoy doing it and if you keep doing it, you're most of the way there."

"Never think that any piece of time is too small to get your artwork done."

Incidentally, Eric has one other bit of information to share with his readers. There is a secret story in *Zoom Upstream*; it's written in code on the endpapers. He suggests that interested sleuths solve the upper left-hand side of the puzzle for a clue to the code. Happy hunting!

DO IT YOURSELF!

When Eric Beddows is happy with his drawings, he uses tracing paper to keep the best parts, then transfers them onto good paper. He suggests you draw something once — a dragon, for instance — then rip off its head, legs and tail. (You can do this with a photocopy instead of your original drawing if you'd like.) Then move the pieces around on a blank sheet of paper and you'll find it gives you all kinds of surprising ideas, positions and postures. When you find one you like, tape the pieces down and trace the whole thing onto tracing paper. Then repeat the process with that drawing, and so on. The main thing is not to get too attached to your own drawing, and to try new things.

Philippe Béha

SELECTED TITLES

Born:
January 1, 1950, in
Casablanca, Morocco

Home:
Montreal, Quebec

Philippe Béha can't seem to find enough time to illustrate. After a busy eight-hour day in his studio, he takes a break to spend the evening with his wife and daughters; then, while his family sleeps, he's back at his table, often working right through the night. Needless to say, Philippe does not need a lot of sleep!

It's no wonder, though, that he keeps such long hours. Philippe likes to have as many as ten projects on the go, and in the twenty years he's been a professional illustrator he has done illustrations for more than 100 books!

Describing himself as an excited child, Philippe quickly becomes absorbed in each new project. He works fast, taking only a couple of hours to complete even his most complex illustrations. He even completed the pictures for his book *What Do the Fairies Do with All Those Teeth?* in what is surely a record-breaking two days! That includes the rough sketches *and* all of the paintings! Fantastic feats like this make some of his friends wonder if he's from another planet.

Philippe doesn't concentrate his efforts only on illustrating for kids, though. His vibrant illustrations have found their place in posters, advertisements and magazines for readers of all ages.

SECRET RECIPES

Philippe is known for his ability to draw in many different styles. He works in watercolours, but it's what he mixes with his paints that makes his technique so unusual. "At first, I just worked with water, but later I began experimenting with whatever

I found around the house. I'll often spend the entire night in the kitchen trying different mixtures. Sometimes nothing comes of it, but once in a while I hit something great. If it suits the illustration, I'll use it once, maybe twice, and then never use it again."

Philippe won't reveal any of his special secret recipes, but teases that it could be anything from eggs to orange juice! He rarely uses the same combination more than twice because each of his books is so different that it simply wouldn't look right. "Sometimes I can use the same thing, but generally I want to try new things. If it surprises me, I know it will surprise my readers."

His favourite part of doing an illustration is thinking up the ideas, Philippe says, and he explains that the faster they come, the better they are. "It's like a game. I start and I say, in ten minutes I must have a good concept." He almost always comes up with one. After years of practice and so many projects, Philippe says some of the things he comes up with still surprise him!

Philippe will take on just about any project that comes his way, all

the while looking for new challenges and new ways to experiment with style and technique. "You get to a point where nothing scares you — and that makes it fun. There isn't a challenge I won't take on. Time, experience and success give you a certain self-assurance. Once you're committed, you'll always find a way."

"In illustration you can make anything happen. Unlike photography, you don't need a set-up, a camera or an assistant. All you need is a good idea, something to draw with, and you can create anything you want."

DO IT YOURSELF!

Take some inspiration from Philippe Béha's midnight concoctions and experiment by mixing different things into your watercolour paints. You could, for instance, try sand, corn starch, salt or crayon shavings to see how these things alter the colour and texture. Anything goes!

Jo Ellen Bogart

Born:
October 20, 1945, in Houston, Texas, USA

Home:
Guelph, Ontario

When she was a child, Jo Ellen Bogart recalls, her mother encouraged her to make beautiful picture books. Still, Jo Ellen didn't decide to become an author until she moved to Canada in 1975. More than ten years later, the manuscripts for her books *Dylan's Lullaby* and *Malcolm's Runaway Soap* were accepted for publication by two different editors.

True to her mother's words, Jo Ellen continues to make beautiful books, drawing on her family, friends and especially pets for ideas. "My experience has been that picture book ideas come on their own if I wait patiently and open my mind. Most poems and stories I write take just a few hours. Then weeks later I might pick them up and work on some polishing."

And what about those odd occasions when Jo Ellen decides to play hooky? "I do housework. To put off doing housework, I read or play with my pets. When I'm very restless, I drive out into the country and watch cows and horses and sheep. I love to hear the sounds they make in the quiet, and I *love* to be able to see for long distances. I guess it reminds me of Texas where I grew up."

A REAL ANIMAL LOVER

In fact, Jo Ellen has always enjoyed being around animals, at one time or another sharing her home with a coatimundi named Clyde (look for him in *Sarah Saw a Blue Macaw*), Tortor, an Argentine desert tortoise which runs loose around the house, an African clawed frog named Astro, a chipmunk named Alvin which was rescued from a trap, forty mice, assorted gerbils, guinea pigs, water turtles and the occasional salamander. She even spent time in South America with her zoologist husband, studying creatures of the rainforest and taking pictures which would eventually inspire her book, *Sarah Saw a Blue Macaw*.

Further inspiration for that book came when Jo Ellen was volunteering as a speech therapist in her children's school. There, she and her students would play around with sentences that used irregular verbs in different tenses. "With my mind in that set I heard myself say, Sarah saw a blue macaw. This happens a lot. I hear the title in my head and from that the story will go."

After writing the first draft of a poem that was full of irregular verbs and began with the question, What did Sarah see?, Jo Ellen talked to her editor at Scholastic. Together they decided to change the story from one whose characters lived in a city neighbourhood to one about rainforest animals in their natural environment. Jo Ellen stuck with the irregular verbs and with her question and answer format, but the fact that she could no longer talk about bicycles and other civilized things made finding rhyming words a lot trickier. "Every restriction made the target smaller. It was like an enormous puzzle."

But puzzle it out she did, managing to achieve a personal goal along the way — creating a book that would be translated into Spanish, a language she has herself studied. "Sometimes it's good to be flexible. We worked together and came up with a good book."

Jo Ellen has two pieces of advice for interested young authors. The first is to read as much as you can. "Reading provides such a wonderful supply of ideas and language and of other people's thoughts and experiences."

The second piece of advice is to "mull over" what you have seen or read or done or felt.

"Mulling is rolling around words and images in your head. From the outside, it looks a lot like daydreaming. The next step might be to mull on paper. Getting your own thoughts down where you can look at them again is good. Sooner or later something good, something you really like, will appear in these writings."

When asked to describe her favourite part of writing stories and poems, Jo Ellen replies, "My favourite part is the sheer enjoyment of making something up and liking it. The next good part is having people say that *they* like what I have written. Being able to make a career of writing and have a lot of freedom with my time is wonderful." Though she admits, "Not having regular daily contact with people in a working environment can be lonely."

> *"Making a story happen is like filling an empty space. There was nothing there before you started and when you finish, there is something."*

DO IT YOURSELF!

Here's a tall-tale writing idea from Jo Ellen Bogart. Write a letter to an imaginary friend to tell that friend what's happening in your life — or in your cousin's life, or your dog's life, or your iguana's life (even if you don't have an iguana). If the truth needs rearranging, do it. If made-up parts make the story better, add them. Throw your ingredients into the pot and stir!

Paulette Bourgeois

SELECTED TITLES

Born:
July 20, 1951, in Winnipeg, Manitoba

Home:
Toronto, Ontario

Paulette Bourgeois recalls, "I was once told by my grade ten English teacher that I could write well, and I've never forgotten it. I wonder what would have happened if somebody had said I could play basketball well!"

Although she says this in jest — Paulette insists she's too short to play basketball! — she does suspect that when she was in school, she spent too much time with her nose in a book and not enough time trying other things, particularly athletic things.

But maybe all of that reading was the thing that got her hooked on writing in the first place. Paulette has made quite a name for herself by writing picture book stories about her shy turtle friend, Franklin, but she's also created all sorts of kid-friendly information

books on everything from dirt to apples. "I love finding out things. I have research and interviewing skills and I like to use them."

Paulette describes her first publishing experience this way: "It was exciting to have a book to send, disappointing when I received my first six rejections, thrilling to have it accepted and frustrating to have to keep on working at it."

WRITING BEGETS WRITING

She *does* keep working at it, though. "Writing begets writing!" says Paulette. So, even when she's really struggling with a piece, Paulette stays in her office, where she reads or works on one of the other two or three projects she has going. "Sometimes, though, if I find I'm blocked on something for days and days and days on end, I seriously question whether I know where I'm going in the story and whether the story is worth writing."

Often Paulette has help in making these initial decisions. "Each of my nonfiction topics is suggested by my publisher. Then I decide on the outline, on how I'm going to research it and what's going to be included. I try to think about what I would have wanted to know about the subject when I was a kid."

When she's working on a new nonfiction book, Paulette requires about four months just to do the research, which isn't surprising given the kinds of questions she needs to answer. "In *The Amazing Dirt Book*, I had to answer the question: Do people ever eat dirt and why? That was a tricky one. But I'm very lucky to have a research library close by which is connected by computer to a large data base. I asked the librarian to do the search for me, then I got a lot of journals and articles to read about that topic." (For those of you who are curious, people from more than two hundred cultures eat dirt. You'll have to read Paulette's book to learn more about dirt eating, a practice she doesn't recommend!)

When it's time to begin writing, Paulette believes in being organized. "I spend at least a week making a detailed outline and then I work to the outline. I rarely stray and I do at least one major and two or three minor revisions. Then we get experts to read the book and there's usually one more major edit required."

Paulette says that the ideas for her Franklin books come from her own childhood memories — how she felt, how she reacted — but they also come from overhearing conversations or from reading books, magazines and newspapers.

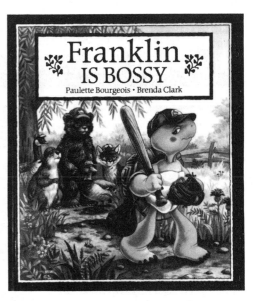

"Having somebody that you admire and respect tell you that you've done something well makes an enormous impact."

Franklin was not inspired by a pet turtle, as Paulette has never had a turtle of her own.

"Most of my work is getting ideas, and that I do sitting in front of a fire or in the summer at my cottage where I look out at the ocean and the sand dunes. Also, it's amazing the number of ideas I get going to the symphony. I guess listening to the music jogs ideas. It's just a peaceful time to think." In fact, Paulette is so serious about the inspiration music gives her that she doesn't listen to music while she works, for fear that too many ideas will come through and make it hard for her to focus.

People often say to Paulette, Writing must be so hard because you're alone all the time. But that couldn't be farther from the truth. "I think people generally forget that you choose to spend time alone. I like it — I think I need it."

DO IT YOURSELF!

If you have trouble ending your stories, why not start your story at the end? Paulette Bourgeois suggests you make up a great last line and then work backwards, asking yourself questions like: How could this happen? Whom did this happen to? What were those characters like?

Ron Broda

SELECTED TITLES

The Little Crooked Christmas Tree
1990

Waters
1993

Born:
May 26, 1954, in New Hamburg, Ontario

Home:
Sarnia, Ontario

The sixth child in a family of eleven children, Ron Broda was not a great reader when he was in school. In fact, he had so much trouble reading as a kid that he avoided it whenever he could. He preferred instead to pursue the unusual hobby of collecting animals. "I used to be one of those children who, after school, went through bushes chasing anything that would run, or crawl in a hole, or fly. I tried to get as close as I could, thinking I could catch it."

And catch them he did. "I had everything. The most pigeons I had at one time was about 240. And then I had ducks and chickens and rabbits and groundhogs. I kept them *all* as pets."

It may not be a coincidence, then, that Ron does such a great job of sculpting animals in paper.

Even in those early years he was experimenting with the medium, as he fondly recalls cutting out paper cats to decorate the windows for Halloween. "I was a *real* animal person."

HIS OWN PERSONAL STYLE

After putting himself through art college as the drummer in a band, Ron received a gift from a friend: a poster featuring a photograph of an illustration which was made entirely out of paper sculpture. He was so taken with the look of the piece that he decided to experiment with the medium in earnest, and eventually developed his own personal style.

"When I went through college, I thought you were born with a style. None of the teachers ever said you should develop a style and try different things. Sooner or later, though, you try everything and you play with everything and there's suddenly one medium that you enjoy."

When kids ask Ron: How did you do that? he finds it hard to provide them with a detailed answer. His quick explanation of how he works with paper is: "I cut and fold it with my hands, and curl it with different instruments like scissors."

But much more than that is involved creating the stunning three-dimensional pieces that make up Ron's books. He's always fine-tuning his craft and even uses materials other than paper on occasion to achieve a desired effect. For instance, in his book *Waters*, Ron used a glue gun and cut up pieces of acetate to make spider's webs, melting snow and icicles. When the pieces were photographed for the book, the lights glistened through the built-up acetate and made his pictures seem more realistic.

Instead of buying paper in hundreds of different colours, Ron usually begins with plain white watercolour paper. Then he tints the paper with watercolour paints, creating exactly the colours he wants. This also makes it possible for him to paint details like eyes on his creatures when he's finished sculpting.

A small picture can take as long as twelve hours to do. So when Ron is working on a particularly difficult piece, he's careful not to let himself get overwhelmed. "I treat it as a puzzle, doing one piece at a time. If I'm not really into it one day, I'll get at least one piece done and the next day I'll get

another piece done, and before you know it I'm getting a lot of pieces done and two weeks are gone and it's almost finished."

Ron draws sketches for the entire book first. Then he begins the paper sculpture, starting with the pages that excite him the least, and saving his favourites for last. This keeps him enthusiastic about the job right up until it's finished. "You've got to keep that positive feeling going all the time!"

Ron Broda on developing a style: "Don't think, I haven't got it yet and it's getting to that time when I'll need it. It will come."

DO IT YOURSELF!

Ron Broda suggests you keep a sketchbook and draw for at least five minutes, but no more than ten minutes, every day. It won't be hard to get in the habit because it's such a short time to work, but over time it will make a big difference in helping you to develop your own personal style.

Margaret Buffie

Born:
March 29, 1945, in Winnipeg,
Manitoba

Home:
Winnipeg, Manitoba

"**I** think I always knew that someday I would write a book," Margaret Buffie recalls. "The seed of this ambition was sown by my grade four teacher, Miss Day. I can remember when she handed me back one of my stories; she told me she was sure I would be a writer some day and that stuck in my brain. I never forgot her enthusiastic encouragement. After she said that, I always believed that I could do it."

That belief in herself has taken Margaret a long way. Her first book was accepted by a publisher just two weeks after it was submitted, which is possibly an industry record! "The whole experience was both frightening and terribly exciting. In fact, I jumped up and down after I hung up the phone and I put my back out for two days. It was an exquisite pain!"

But while Margaret was confident about writing from the beginning, she was not prepared for editing. "The thing I had to do before I would be able to have the book published was to work with an editor and shorten the book by about fifty pages, and that was a really terrifying prospect. But I was encouraged and applauded by both my editor and my publisher throughout the whole process. It's funny, when I finally saw the finished books I was in absolute awe and I remember asking myself: Who did this? I really didn't think I could have done it myself!"

Margaret has developed a number of techniques for revising her work, but one of the most important is used to develop dialogue. "Sometimes the changes come easily, but sometimes I have to 'talk' with my characters and let them have a say in where exactly I've gone wrong. This happens during the revision process. If your characters aren't saying the right things, then you have to get to know them a little bit better and let them say what they want to say. If something is stilted or unnatural, then you know *your* words are shaping it and *not* the characters'."

Readers often ask Margaret if she plans to write other books using the same characters. To which Margaret replies, "*The Guardian Circle* has an ending that offers a possible sequel, but I've found that sequels to movies and to other books are often a disappointment, so I think that I'll only do a sequel to *The Guardian Circle* if I get a new idea that will be as strong and full of action as the first book and if I feel strongly compelled to spend a year writing it."

In the meantime, however, there are many more things to write about; Margaret never seems to run out of ideas. "If anything, I wish I was three people so I could set us all in front of a computer and say: Okay, here it is. Get going!"

Margaret is tentatively beginning her next novel on the computer, but she still isn't sure that this is the best way for her. "My first draft up until now has always been done in longhand — which is maybe why it takes me a year and a half to write a book! There seems to be some real connection between my brain and my hand — it may have to do with the fact that I'm an artist. Then I move on to the computer for the next few drafts of the manuscript."

ON A ROLL

"I definitely have a tendency to procrastinate, but once I do bypass all of these things and sit down and get to work, it's very hard to take a break. I usually become so involved in it. There are many days when the story that I'm working on is really going so well that I sit down at nine and I have to be dragged away from it. I even eat my lunch over the keyboard!"

"I always find it intriguing to ask people where they get their ideas from."

DO IT YOURSELF!

Plan and prepare a combination diary/sketchbook just like Frances Rain's daughter did in Margaret Buffie's book *Who Is Frances Rain?* You could either create one for Frances Rain's daughter based on the information you collect from the book, or you could create one for yourself, collecting information and pictures over a number of months or years.

Perhaps part of the reason Margaret becomes so involved in her work is that she identifies so much with the subject matter. The setting for Margaret's first book, *Who Is Frances Rain?* was based on her own cottage experiences. "I had gone to a cottage like Gran's all of my life, and because I'd painted and photographed it so much over the years I really felt that I knew what it smelt like and what it looked like. Because it was such an important part of my life experience, I really wanted to write a book about it."

The rest of Margaret's inspiration for *Who Is Frances Rain?* came when she was digging around on an island near that same cottage. As she worked to clear the land of an old garbage dump, she came across a jug containing an old pair of spectacles and the question came to her: What would happen if I put them on and was able to look into the past?

From that one question an entire story evolved. So the next time you run out of ideas, you may want to consider the very same thing: Ask *yourself* a question to get the ball rolling.

Brenda Clark

Born:
February 10, 1955, in Toronto, Ontario

Home:
Nestleton, Ontario

Looking back on her childhood, Brenda Clark comments, "I didn't read enough and I have to make up for it now. Reading is good because you get all these images in your mind and it just helps you draw better. Take my word for it — it works!"

What little reading Brenda *did* do when she was young happened at school. "I really liked the school readers. I remember looking at those pictures and wondering about who drew them. I was actually inspired by those first readers, believe it or not."

And what came next for this artist who had spent her early years gazing at the pictures in her school readers? Why, the job of illustrating readers herself, of course! "My first published pieces were for readers. Which was, for me, a dream come true. It was something I'd always wondered about. It was really exciting to see something printed and I still get that same feeling after all these years."

Brenda admits that, despite the thrill of seeing her work in print, she is sometimes disappointed by the way the colours in her paintings change when they're printed in books. She has, however, over the years found ways to get around this common illustrator's complaint. "When I first started out, I experimented with pencil crayons and chalks and different coloured papers, but I found that for me watercolours reproduced the brightest. I don't use watercolours like a watercolourist. I use water really sparingly, so it's mostly just the colour you see. I build up from the lightest colours to the darkest colours. This is called glazing."

Brenda believes in being prepared when she begins a new project. "I love doing research, I really do. And I think it probably helps a lot when I get projects like *Little Fingerling*, for instance. I needed to portray accurately the Japanese lifestyle of long ago and I couldn't make that up. So I did months of research at the Royal Ontario Museum. They have a Far East library there, so I had access to actual Japanese art and artifacts throughout the whole nine months that it took me to do the book. There were two librarians there who specialized in the language and in the culture and they helped me whenever I had any questions. I gave them credit at the beginning of the book."

In addition to careful research, Brenda values feedback from a number of sources. Once, she received a letter from a boy who wanted to know why the ice in the plastic bag in Sadie and the Snowman didn't look like ice. In the book, Sadie wants to keep her snowman over the summer, so she puts her melted friend in the freezer, and the following winter takes the bag of ice out to make a new snowman. "I guess I didn't have the technical ability at that time. He was perfectly right. I made it look like snow instead of ice. It should have been more transparent."

Franklin's character, too, took a lot of reworking. Says Brenda, "At first he didn't look like a turtle. When I first brought him in I was told he looked sort of like a parrot or a lizard. So I literally had to go back to the drawing board and give him more appeal. I added a few human expressions and characteristics so he would stand out from your regular everyday turtle."

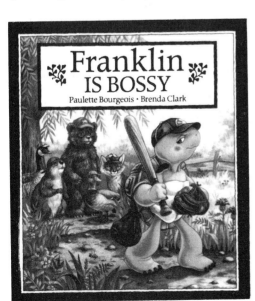

Brenda often looks to her publisher and the book's author for thoughts on her drawings. "They go over them and I just wait to see what their comments are. I hope they have suggestions because I'm always looking for something fresh and because it's hard for one person to see everything. Some of the changes that they suggest may not seem appropriate to me at first, but if I think about them or if I give them a try, often I'm surprised by the improvement."

Brenda's words of advice for people interested in becoming professional illustrators are: "Pretend your mind is a camera and click pictures every chance you get. Try and remember things like patterns, shapes and colours, and keep a sketchbook handy at all times. Then go through your sketchbook every once in a while and pick out your very best sketches. Keep them aside in a portfolio and look back at it and see how much you've improved. It will give you the incentive to keep at it because you *will* see improvement."

Brenda Clark's books are available to children all around the world. "I never dreamed my illustrations would be seen by so many people. Some of the titles are even seen in faraway places like Japan and Australia, Belgium and Great Britain, and I often wonder what the children in Kyoto or Sydney think of Franklin the turtle."

"I don't believe there's any such thing as making a mistake, but I do believe in changes."

DO IT YOURSELF!

A little planning can go a long way. Brenda Clark suggests that before you do the pictures for a book you've written, you work out all the bugs by doing some thumbnail sketches. (Thumbnail sketches are just very small rough drawings of the pictures you plan to do.) Sketch each picture in a number of different ways: from a bird's eye view, from a worm's eye view, from far away or close up. Thumbnail sketches save you from wasting time or paper on angles and ideas that don't work, giving you more time to work on your final illustrations.

Lyn Cook

Born:
May 4, 1918, in Weston, Ontario

Home:
Scarborough, Ontario

Lyn Cook was only seven years old when she found the secret hole in the lilac hedge. There she would retreat with her reading or her writing, remaining hidden until she was discovered. But reading wasn't always a secretive thing for Lyn. Although her family lived in the country where there was no library, books were always cherished. "One of the things my father did for us was that he brought us a very old-fashioned encyclopedia called *The Book of Knowledge*. It had wonderful stories in it. It had condensations of famous books; it had myths and legends; it had poetry — we devoured those. It was a wonderful thing."

In fact, reading was one of Lyn's two favourite activities. She still remembers the occasions when her books were taken away. "If you mis-behaved, the punishment was that you were to go to your room, where you were deprived of what you liked the most. Today, I suppose, you would be deprived of watching TV."

Her second love was story-telling. "In my two-room country school, there was a wonderful teacher called Miss Smiley. She saw in me the need to tell stories and the ability to do it, and she used to have me up to tell them. Mind you, I was the shyest child in the world, but when I got up there I totally forgot my shyness and was a storyteller. Sometimes I told stories from the books that I had read, and sometimes while I was doing this I also changed the story if I didn't like the middle or the end, and that way started being my own creator.

"When I went to high school that was the first time, really, that I met a library, and I became so entranced with it that I became a library assistant right then and there. I was determined I was going to be surrounded by those books."

After university, Lyn continued her work among the stacks, as the sole librarian for fifteen schools in a library on top of a Loblaws store. And somehow, with a job and a young family, Lyn managed to begin writing her first book.

WAITING FOR THE IDEAS

"I never start writing the actual book until all of the ideas are in — until I'm fully aware of what is going to happen in the book." But for Lyn this isn't always a speedy process.

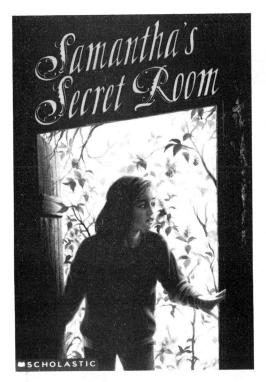

"I have to wait until a story comes. It will start with something that happened yesterday, or it could have happened years ago, and that plants a seed in my mind and the story starts to grow. It's as if it's a magnet; ideas come to join that idea. It could happen suddenly when you're putting the dishes in the dishwasher, or you could hear somebody say something. It just seems as if once the creative mind is open, then other pieces of the jigsaw come to fit in. Sometimes, I feel that it's as if it all happened before and I'm remembering it, but not in sequence. And then I see it in sequence when it's finished."

Lyn's advice for authors who are looking for something to write about is to start with an incident that you cannot forget, and go from there. So many of her own books are based on just those kinds of memories. For instance, her secret hiding place in the hedge became the basis for her book *Samantha's Secret Room*, and her novels *The Secret of Willow Castle*, *The Road to Kip's Cove* and *The Magical Miss Mittens* are all set in old houses which were inspired by one of her own childhood fascinations. "Across the road from us in a great empty field were two houses that we called the brown houses. They were empty — they were really derelict — and we filled them, of course, with ghosts and with skeletons. We were always daring one another to go in and nobody dared."

Lyn spends more time refining her writing than she actually does writing. Whenever possible she likes to take a break between drafts. "I find that if you leave your work aside for a little while, the mistakes become much clearer — if you can afford the time to do that. Perhaps work on something else. When you go back, you'll find things are more glaringly obvious; things that you felt were all right in the first place, suddenly you'll see that they aren't."

Lyn also welcomes her editor's input as she continues the revision process, but insists on doing the actual revisions herself. "I won't allow anyone to do my work for me. The work of an editor is not to write for you, but to draw out of you what is really in there all the time."

"I don't think you choose writing; I think writing and storytelling choose you. In other words, I believe I was born telling stories."

DO IT YOURSELF!

Lyn Cook has discovered all kinds of ideas for her books by learning about her family history and about the history of Canada. Inquire into your own family or community history and write a story based on what you've learned.

Sylvie Daigneault

SELECTED TITLES

 Illustrations only.

Born:
November 28, 1952, in Montreal, Quebec

Home:
Toronto, Ontario

"**W**hen I was really young I remember cutting myself little tiny pieces of paper and making a book. Then I pretended that I was writing. In fact, I was sort of drawing writing because I would go 'curl, curl, curl, space' and I did the whole book like that. I was really proud of my book. I used pencil crayons when I made it."

Years later, Sylvie attended a convent school in Montreal. She says, "A nice convent with Italian nuns. At this school everything was oriented to art and performance and music. The art teacher there told me she thought I had a special talent with drawing, and said I could come to the art class and draw whatever I wanted, whenever I had free time. This was in grades two, three and four, so the encouragement started early."

LOOKING AT EVERY ANGLE

After so many years of practice, Sylvie has learned the importance of paying close attention to detail. "I do a lot of research. I go to the library and sometimes I'll take out a hundred pictures for one book. Even though I know how to draw things like flowers, I like to go and look at references because I think your drawings get better when you have more information; otherwise you tend to draw everything the same way. You get comfortable about drawing a dog a certain way or drawing a cat a certain way, and you just stick to it. Sometimes I even have five pictures for the same animal because I want to know how long the tail is and in one picture the tail is not there.

"I usually spend about a day per linear [original pencil drawing] and the finished art goes between two and four days. I do all of the linears in order because a story has a momentum. It's like reading a book or watching a movie; I don't want to watch the middle of the movie and then go back to the beginning. I usually do the cover last because the cover is supposed to reflect what's inside, and by the time I've done all of the pages, I'm totally familiar with all of the characters and the mood."

Although she began her career using paint as her medium, Sylvie has been using pencil crayons to do her illustrations for more than fifteen years. "I decided one day to go to pencils because it was an easy medium to carry around and it has such a wide variety of colours. I think they also appeal to me because they almost look like sticks of candy."

But using pencil has its own challenges. The colour and texture of the paper, for instance, become really important. Sylvie says, "For *Mama's Bed* I got a whole bunch of cream paper and when all the linears had been done and I'd started colouring, I didn't like the texture. I was not happy at all about the way the pencil was responding with the paper. And I trashed everything and went back and I bought another kind of paper. Paper really changes pencil and I change paper often, depending on what I want to achieve." If you look closely at *Sarah Saw a Blue Macaw*, for example, you can see that every page was drawn on a different paper!

When she finally does achieve a look she likes, Sylvie looks for a

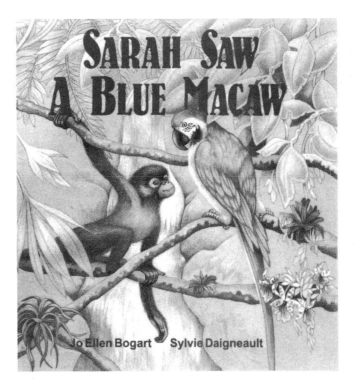

second opinion. "My husband is an illustrator, so I'll often show him my sketches and ask what he thinks. You get so close to what you do, you don't quite see if there's something wrong. I like to have another opinion."

"The best way to achieve something unique and strong is by being yourself. It's good to be influenced by other people, but I think it's best to reach a place where you feel really comfortable because it's your work and there's nobody else quite like you."

"I like to push my knowledge of drawing."

DO IT YOURSELF!

Sylvie Daigneault suggests you look at a friend, a pet or even a view — then turn away from your subject and try to draw from memory what you've seen.

Christiane Duchesne

SELECTED TITLES

Gaspard ou le chemin des montagnes
1984

 Quel beau petit!
1986

 Ah! ces oiseaux
1986

Un dessin pour Tara
1989

Le voyage de Benjamin
1990

La vraie histoire du chien de Clara Vic
(Governor General's Literary Award)
1990

Bibitsa, ou, l'étrange voyage de Clara Vic
(Mr. Christie's™ Book Award)
1991

L'été des tordus
1992

Victor
(Governor General's Literary Award)
1992

La 42ᵉ soeur de Bébert
(Mr. Christie's™ Book Award)
1993

 Adapted from the English.

Born:
August 12, 1949, in Montreal, Quebec

Home:
Montreal, Quebec

When Christiane Duchesne was little, she read absolutely everything she could get her hands on. She read novels, storybooks, her parents' magazines, the dictionary — everything. And she always went to sleep with a book in her hands. Perhaps it was the diversity of this early reading material that prompted her to try so many different kinds of writing. "I think I've tried my hand at every genre, for work and also for pleasure: stories, novels, translations, songs, plays, scripts and all the writing work and research that would earn me a living."

In fact, since she began working as a writer fourteen years ago, Christiane has translated about 400 titles and published eighteen original books for children, seven of which she also illustrated.

For Christiane, the writing profession is ideal because it permits such a great amount of freedom — after all, how many people can do their jobs with just a pencil and a paper napkin? But Christiane wasn't always so sure of the path she would take. "I never actually decided to 'become an author.' I had always written for my own enjoyment, but I never believed that I could write for a living; the proof of which is in the fact that I went to study industrial design at an architectural college. But for whatever reason, by chance or by destiny, it was writing that got the upper hand."

And now writing is what Christiane does every day. "I never let myself get stopped by writer's block. If the ideas aren't coming,

I just do something else. And since I have a million things to do, there are plenty to chose from."

A MILLION THINGS TO DO

Christiane really does seem to have a million things to do, and because she specializes in a number of different areas, each job is different. "This week, for example, I took three days to write a script for the next show at the Montreal planetarium; I recorded a series of broadcasts on legends and music for Radio Canada; I gave an hour-long course on writing and radio; and I worked on a book I'm doing for Québec/Amérique. I also started writing a Christmas story and I worked out plans for a novel in my head."

With all of that on the go, there isn't much time for Christiane to do anything else. She has done a fair bit of travelling, though, and when she can fit it into her schedule, Christiane enjoys talking to kids.

She recalls being invited to talk to a group of grade two students at a local library. The group arrived with a substitute teacher who didn't seem to know anything about the visit, and it soon became obvious to Christiane that the students were getting more and more restless. After a time, one little girl stood and asked when the show was supposed to begin. Apparently, because the substitute teacher had not been specific about the kind of show they would be attending, the

"Everyone can make stories; it isn't just the privilege of authors."

class assumed they were going to see marionettes or some other fabulous spectacle that Christiane could not provide. It made for an awkward visit indeed, and now she's careful to tell her audiences up front: "Listen, this may be very, very dull, but the show is me!" This description actually isn't too far off the mark, because with her many skills Christiane Duchesne really is a kind of one-person show!

DO IT YOURSELF!

To do Christiane's activity you'll need a partner. Use a dictionary to make a list of ten words each, which are new to you. Then exchange papers and, without looking up the definitions of the words, write a short story using every word on your partner's list. The challenging part is making up meanings for all of those words. Share your stories, and only then look up the real definitions.

Eugenie Fernandes

 Illustrations only.

Born:
September 25, 1943, in Huntington, New York, USA

Home:
Peterborough, Ontario

The Golden Book series was started the year before Eugenie Fernandes was born, and those were the books she loved when she was growing up, reading them mostly for the art. Some years later, continuing her relationship with the series, Eugenie actually wrote and illustrated Golden Books of her own and when they were published, she was understandably thrilled. "I got a big kick out of looking in the backs of the Golden Books because they have a list of their classics. And there I was with these illustrators that I really loved."

Eugenie began her career as an illustrator when a co-worker at the greeting card company where she was working suggested she talk to an agent. Eugenie followed this advice and soon published a story which she now describes as "just horrible." The story was called *Wicked Dishrag* and it was about a nasty little girl who dresses up like a witch for Halloween and begins to turn into one for real because she is so good at it.

"I did a lot of forgettable little cheap books, but I'm really grateful for those because I didn't come out of art school like Nicola Bayley — she is just marvellous. I had to struggle along until I got to be a little bit better."

IT HAS TO SOUND GOOD

Part of that struggle involves fine-tuning the language of her stories. "It has to sound good and not just be an interesting story; the words have to feel good in your mouth. There's a rhythm — not a rhyme — in the sentence structure. Sometimes when I'm writing I'll have a word that needs to be two syllables and the word I've written is only one syllable. So then I'll go searching around for a word with the right number of syllables in it so that it works with my cadence, my voice."

For as long as she can remember, Eugenie has loved the outdoors. As a child she lived near the beach. "In the summertime I was always up a tree or at the beach or under the water. Those were the three places you could find me."

Today, you can find Eugenie in her studio overlooking a lake. Weather permitting, she rises before the sun and sits by the water to think. Readers will recognize Eugenie's continuing fascination with water and nature popping up in such books as *Waves in the Bathtub* and *The Tree that Grew to the Moon*.

Eugenie says, "I always like to have a story in the back of my mind." She goes on to explain that she usually has two or three ideas "waiting" for her to have time to work on them. "When I go to bed at night, I think about stories and write them in my head. And by the time I have the story written — because I've done it in my head — I usually have it memorized."

Eugenie believes there are three important things to remember when you are writing a story. First and foremost, you should write what you know because a story has to have your feelings in it. "If your dog got run over, write about that. If you have a wonderful tree house where you like to hide, write about that."

Second, there has to be some tension. "Even in a happy story like *Waves in the Bathtub* there's a bit of tension in the mother wanting Kady to scrub her toes!"

Eugenie Fernandes

Third, never give up. Eugenie recalls the words of her young fans, which she says she hangs on to and repeats to herself whenever she's feeling discouraged, but it takes more than that to stay happy in this business.

Eugenie says that you shouldn't write books unless you love it, "because it's very discouraging in the beginning. Before I was doing books professionally I would make books anyway — for nobody, for no reason. I was constantly writing stories and making little books. Anyone going into the business has to be quite determined and able to get up again when publishers say: Don't call us. We'll call you."

"I think I lived the stories when I was a child."

DO IT YOURSELF!

Eugenie Fernandes can look at a piece of driftwood and see a horse, or a fish or a mermaid. She suggests that you find a stick or a stone and, once you've decided what it reminds you of, paint it to enhance the resemblance.

Laszlo Gal

 Illustrations only.

Born:
February 18, 1933, in Budapest, Hungary

Home:
Willowdale, Ontario

When Laszlo Gal moved to Canada from Hungary in 1956, there was no children's publishing industry here to speak of. He spoke no English at all, but he managed to find a job working at the CBC. Despite this unlikely beginning, Laszlo was soon to fall into the world of children's books, because there were two other important influences at work. "I knew how to draw a little bit here and there," he says, *and* he was raised on fairy tales. Laszlo is the youngest of six children, and as a boy he enjoyed the stories told to him by his sister Irene, who was ten years his elder.

And so, nearly twenty-two years later, and without any plans as to what he would do with them, Laszlo decided to include a number of children's book illustrations in his art portfolio. One summer, on a trip to Italy with his wife, he began to search for advertising agencies that would look at his work. In Milan, they bumped into a young priest who was coming out of a cathedral. They asked him for directions, and he introduced them to a man he knew personally — a man who would eventually put Laszlo in touch with the editor-in-chief of one of the largest publishing houses in Europe, Mondadori. Coincidentally, Mondadori had only just begun its children's publishing department when Laszlo arrived, and in 1964 he became one of their first illustrators.

Laszlo later moved back to Europe, where he illustrated books for children for four years. Then he returned to Canada where he met author Janet Lunn. She asked him to do a book with her, and together they worked on *The Twelve Dancing Princesses* for nearly three years.

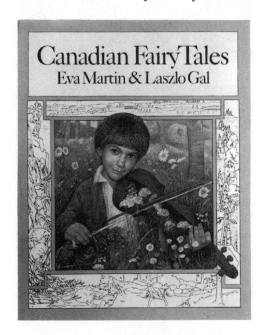

Canadian FairyTales
Eva Martin & Laszlo Gal

TWO SPECIAL FACES

"The originals were really huge tableaus. I spent two and a half years on seven illustrations, and those seven illustrations were very, very detailed. Every single figure there was a portrait of my two kids. There are twelve princesses, but I kept alternating the two, and you'll see there really are only two faces repeating each other."

When Laszlo showed those first paintings of oil on paper to an artist friend, he was ridiculed for spending so much time on them. But Laszlo believed that if he were going to be recognized at all for his work as a children's illustrator, it would be for the work he did on this book. He was right. *The Twelve Dancing Princesses* made Laszlo's reputation and won him a Canada Council award.

Part of the reason this first book took so long to illustrate was Laszlo's careful attention to detail. "When you are drawing a human figure, then anybody can criticize you — his arm is too long, his fingers are pointing in the wrong direction, and so on and so on — everybody becomes an art critic as soon as you do illustrations in a realistic way."

Laszlo spends a great deal of time on his preliminary sketches, believing that success comes from 10 percent talent and 90 percent sweat. "I heard a story that Michelangelo burned all his sketches because he didn't want to let people know how much he worked on them. I don't want to compare myself to Michelangelo, but I do a lot of sketches and I do a lot of research for architecture, for costumes and poses. Sometimes I use live models like my daughters, or I

find photographs from which I can create something."

Laszlo notes that fewer sketches are required for books with stylized illustrations, admitting that these allow him to be freer with his interpretations; for instance, it took him only three months to complete the eighteen illustrations he did for his book *The Moon and the Oyster.* Laszlo was comfortable playing with his style for this book because, as he says, "There are no human figures in it. You don't have to be that careful if you are drawing an octopus. The only thing you have to make sure of is that he has eight feet!"

When he's asked if he likes what he does, Laszlo replies, "I love it. It's almost like an obsession with me. I have a job at the CBC and the books I'm illustrating I'm doing in my spare time. If anybody knew what I make on these illustrations they would laugh in my face. In the beginning I probably made ten, fifteen or twenty cents an hour when the minimum wage was three or four dollars. And I don't think I make more than a dollar an hour right now. It's just insanity that anybody would do such a thing!" But then again, perhaps it's a labour of love!

"Ideas come when one starts to work on the paper. As you see the lines, as you impose one drawing on top of the other, your ideas slowly accumulate."

DO IT YOURSELF!

Laszlo Gal uses his daughters as models for his drawings. Why not ask a friend to pose for you the next time you draw a picture of a person?

Marie-Louise Gay

SELECTED TITLES

Drôle d'école
(Canada Council Children's Literature Prize)
1984

 Lizzy's Lion
(Canada Council Children's Literature Prize)
1984

Moonbeam on a Cat's Ear
(Amelia Frances Howard-Gibbon Illustrator's Award)
1986

Rainy Day Magic
(Amelia Frances Howard-Gibbon Illustrator's Award, Governor General's Literary Award)
1987

Angel and the Polar Bear
1988

Fat Charlie's Circus
1989

Willy Nilly
1990

Mademoiselle Moon
1992

Rabbit Blue
1993

Midnight Mimi
1994

 Illustrations only.

Born:
June 17, 1952, in Quebec City, Quebec

Home:
Outremont, Quebec

As Marie-Louise Gay recalls her childhood, "I was a constant reader — we're talking five to seven books a week. My parents would take me to the library on Saturdays and I would get a pile of books. I would go right through them and next Saturday I was back again. I had a book in front of me all the time."

Marie-Louise started drawing professionally when she was eighteen years old. "I was an editorial illustrator and a cartoon illustrator. I had been doing illustration for at least five years when I started illustrating a few books for children. At that point, a desire came up to write my own stories because I found that I liked to be able to play around with the words and the images so they'd influence each other. When you have a set story you can't necessarily do that. It's sort of like going around with one eye closed. So I decided I would open up a bit and try writing — and it worked."

Because she was already working as an art director in a publishing house when she submitted her first story and illustrations, Marie-Louise knew all about what was involved in publishing books. "What was exciting to me was seeing people read my book for the first time and realizing that I had done something that would last and that would be read over and over again. Because before that I was a commercial illustrator. I would illustrate for magazines and stuff like that, which is really temporary. People wrap up their potato peels in your illustrations. But the impact you could have by illustrating and writing a book! It would hang around; it would go into libraries; kids would borrow it; kids would lend it to their friends. I had finally found something that was enduring."

Marie-Louise uses pen and ink, watercolours and dyes to do her illustrations. And even though much of what she draws appears to be fanciful, she actually does do a lot of research.

"Since my books are very whimsical, there's not a lot of normal research involved. To give you an example, when I worked on Mademoiselle Moon, which is highly imaginative, I did research for moon and sun words — words that would make word plays in my text. Then I looked up different ways the moon and the sun have been illustrated throughout the years in all different types of things — old encyclopedias, post cards — just to influence my drawing and my perspective of seeing the sun and the moon. If I was to show you the things I used, you wouldn't see any relationship with the way I draw, but they're reference points."

HER OWN SPECIAL STYLE

"Now, if I talk about a book like *Rainy Day Magic*, where you have the huge tiger and the whale, I went and got photographs of the animals and then I started deforming them into my style. So you have a tiger who *looks* like a tiger, but his paws are small and his head's very big. To me it's always really important to realize that even if I draw these strange looking animals or people, that underneath, in my mind, they really have bones and must be able to move around. You want the book to be consistent so you'll recognize the hero or the animal throughout the book. You have to understand how the animal or the hero is made underneath."

"Don't copy anyone else. Draw what you see and develop your own style. Originality is the most important thing."

Marie-Louise offers this advice to young people interested in becoming authors and illustrators: "Keep your eyes open all the time. That's when you get your ideas. Look around you and see how people walk and how dogs sniff trees, how flowers look in a certain light and how people move. Listen to songs and stories being told and all of this becomes part of your identity as an author and an illustrator."

DO IT YOURSELF!

Take a tip from Marie-Louise Gay and collect some photographs of real animals. Then combine elements from each to invent an animal that doesn't exist. Draw an environment to suit your creature and decide how it will move and what it will eat. Think carefully before you draw: If you've done an animal with an anteater snout it couldn't be eating watermelons. Of course, if your pictures are as fanciful as Marie-Louise's, maybe it could be!

Phoebe Gilman

 Illustrations only.

Born:
April 4, 1940, in New York City, New York, USA

Home:
Toronto, Ontario

"**N**o one ever inspired me in school," Phoebe Gilman recalls. "In fact, I was the kid in the background who did what she was told, and did nothing particularly extraordinary. I was good at drawing; I was good at writing. But I wasn't the *best* at drawing, and I wasn't the *best* at writing. And I never did anything especially outstanding that a teacher would say: Wow, we have someone special in this class!"

Without encouragement, it was many years before Phoebe decided to try her hand at children's books. Inspiration came one day when, on a walk, her daughter's balloon burst on a tree branch. Phoebe imagined a magic tree blossoming in balloons and began work on her first story, *The Balloon Tree.*

Phoebe fiddled with her story for a long time, treating it as a kind of a hobby, while continuing to work as a professional artist. Finally, she sent it, and her drawings, to publisher after publisher. "I kept getting back rejection slips, but that was okay because it wasn't my 'serious work.' I was just doing it as a lark."

Gradually, though, her book became more important to her. She decided that she really liked writing and illustrating and she loved picture books. And, from that point on, Phoebe wouldn't take no for an answer. "I kept getting all these rejection slips — I got over fifty rejection slips just for *The Balloon Tree* and I was driving my family crazy because every time I'd rewrite it they'd have to listen to the newest version."

PERSISTENCE PAYS OFF

Persistence paid off, though, and in 1984, Scholastic accepted Phoebe's story. "It was months of rewriting and working back and forth, and it was a real education for me on what makes a picture book story work. I didn't know things like it has to fit into thirty-two pages and you've got to leave enough room for pictures in those thirty-two pages. It meant considerable chopping out and editing down."

Why didn't Phoebe, an illustrator by profession, think about the space she would have to leave for her pictures? "I think, at heart, I am a writer who was trained as an artist, because what I'm always drawn to in a book are the words, not the pictures. I will buy picture books for the pictures alone to study them because they're beautiful. But the books I love, I love because of the words."

Even as a child, Phoebe was drawn to books that had no pictures at all (though she confesses to a great love of comic books). She remembers, in particular, searching for good books about adventurous girls. "I read the Nancy Drew series mainly because there were so few books with female heroines — at least Nancy Drew was a hero, of sorts. With all the other books — even the fairy tales — you had to do a kind of mental flip flop to make yourself into the male hero." One can't help but wonder if this is the reason Phoebe decided to make her most loved character, Jillian, a girl.

But that wasn't the real reason Jillian came to be. After her first book was published, Phoebe began to look for ideas for her second book. "I went back to the portfolio I had done when I was looking for work — I had done a lot of samples just using Mother Goose rhymes.

One of the Mother Goose rhymes I had used was 'Gregory Griggs.' 'Gregory, Gregory, Gregory Griggs, / Wore twenty-seven different wigs…' is the way the rhyme goes, and I had a picture of a little boy with a mop on his head who was turning everything in the house into a wig. I thought he looked like a girl, so I decided to change him into one. I looked for a three-syllable girl's name to go with Griggs and all I could come up with was Gillian, spelled with a 'G'. I dropped the 'r' from Griggs, and once Gillian was there, it just took off on its own. We changed the G's to J's because everybody mispronounced it: Gillian Giggs."

Phoebe continues to find ideas everywhere, but she does occasionally go blank. "If I'm having trouble writing or drawing, I try not to run away from it too much, because I find it's the act of writing or the act of drawing that eventually leads me back on track. Running away is dangerous to do, because if you say: I can't work today, and you don't too often, you never work."

"At one point I said: Wait a minute, I love doing this. My kids had all outgrown the picture book stage and I was still going back to that part of the library. They would be mortified: Mom, please, we don't read those kind of books anymore!"

DO IT YOURSELF!

Make a wanted poster for the villain in your favourite book. Draw a picture of the villain and underneath it describe his or her crime, the planned punishment and the reward for his or her capture.

Martyn Godfrey

SELECTED TITLES

Why Just Me?
1989

Can You Teach Me to Pick My Nose?
1990

Monsters in the School
1991

The Great Science Fair Disaster
1992

Meet You in the Sewer
1993

Please Remove Your Elbow from My Ear
1993

My Crazy Book
1994

Just Call Me Boom Boom
1994

Mall Rats
1994

Wild
1994

Born:
April 17, 1949, in Birmingham, England

Home:
St. Albert, Alberta

I n the beginning, writing did not come easily for Martyn Godfrey: "I had to repeat grade three because I couldn't write — I mean, I couldn't put a sentence together to save my life. But now that I look back on it I enjoyed the creative writing aspect of language arts and English."

Martyn Godfrey began writing his first novel more than ten years ago, when he was a teacher. "That was when Thomas Baker was in my class. He was looking for a science fiction novel, and we couldn't find anything for him to read in the library. So, during creative writing class, he suggested that since *he* was writing a story for *me* to read, it would be a good deal if *I* would write a story for *him* to read." Martyn took Thomas up on his offer and about six weeks later that story became the first draft of *The Day the Sky Exploded*.

When he submitted his manuscript to Scholastic and it was accepted, Martyn was surprised. "It was like it wasn't really happening to me. It didn't hit me until I got my first letter from a kid about the book. He was in Nova Scotia and I was in Alberta and I realized: I've connected with this kid 3,000 miles away!"

CONNECTING WITH KIDS

In fact, it's that kind of connection with his readers that Martyn feels makes his books popular with kids. It's so important to him that he ties student involvement into his own revision process. After writing the first draft and two revisions on his Macintosh computer, Martyn likes to put his manuscript aside for a couple of weeks. Then he takes a third look, does a final edit on screen and finally prints it out. Now Martyn reads the whole manuscript to himself. "I sit in front of a wall and read it out loud, imagining I'm a teacher reading it to my class. Sometimes you can write something really well, but it doesn't sound good out loud, and I want my books to be read."

At this point Martyn makes any final adjustments before taking his manuscript to the teachers at one of his test schools, where it will be reviewed by the students. "I'm usually not there when they do it because the kids are more honest that way. Then I go in and listen to what the kids have to say. They spot the inconsistencies and tell me when the stuff isn't funny."

Comments aren't the only things students give Martyn. They also provide him with inspiration for new stories and characters when they meet with him on his many school visits. Even the names of the characters in his books are the names of real people who have written Martyn Godfrey letters.

Martyn talks about one of his favourite letters: "Wally Stutzgummer [namesake of a character in the "Teeny-Wonderful" series] wrote the first fan letter I got

"When I was a teacher, I would teach. I would make my lesson plan for the next day, then I'd go home and spend time with my family. The two lives were separate. Now it never stops. Twenty-four hours a day I'm always writing."

and it went something like: Dear Mr. Godfrey, I read your book *The Vandarian Incident*. I can think of a million reasons why I don't like it, but I will only tell you the first nine. It was signed: Your friend, Wally Stutzgummer."

One can only assume that those nine suggestions were truly helpful, because with four new books on the way and kids everywhere pitching in to help, Martyn Godfrey is still going strong.

DO IT YOURSELF!

When kids ask Martyn how to be funny in a story, he tells them to do three things. One: Create a ridiculous character (some of Martyn's favourites can be found in books by Gordon Korman). Two: Put that character in a ridiculous situation (for example, knocking over a vase on a class trip to the museum). Three: Include slapstick which involves a person in authority who has been written to be unlikeable (for example, the vase falls on the principal's head). Try it yourself!

Ted Harrison

SELECTED TITLES

Children of the Yukon
1977

The Last Horizon
1980

A Northern Alphabet
1982

 The Cremation of Sam McGee
1986

 The Shooting of Dan McGrew
1988

The Blue Raven
1989

O Canada
1993

 Illustrations only.

Born:
August 28, 1926, in Wingate, Durham, England

Home:
Victoria, British Columbia

Ted Harrison began drawing and painting in England at the age of five, but he didn't publish his first book until more than forty years later, long after he'd moved to Canada. "I'd had an exhibition at the Shayne Gallery in Montreal where Tundra saw my work. My simple style seemed to fit in with their ideas. We discussed what the book could be about and we thought of children's games." He went on to complete the book *Children of the Yukon* shortly after Tundra Books approached him, and has been producing colourful picture books for children ever since.

His most recent book, *O Canada*, required a lot of research. Ted says, "I'd been on the Parks Committee for the park centennial of Canada. I was director for the Yukon and I went to nearly every national park in the country. I saw the whole area and I made notes and did sketches and photographs. That was my biggest means of research. I didn't know I was going to do the book then, but it came in mighty handy when I did. I also read lots on the provinces and territories. Libraries were useful, as were the books in my own library. It was a fascinating task and made me realize what an amazing, wonderful country we all live in."

GETTING HIS MIND ON OTHER THINGS

What does Ted do when he runs out of ideas? "I go away and do something different. Recently, I went fishing in the Queen Charlottes and it absolutely rejuvenated me and filled my mind with new ideas." Ted also loves to make

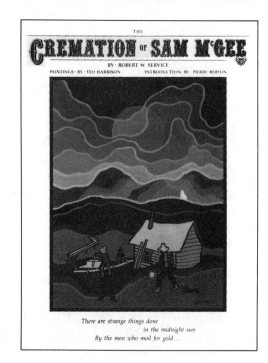

THE
CREMATION OF SAM MCGEE
BY · ROBERT W. SERVICE
PAINTINGS · BY · TED HARRISON   INTRODUCTION · BY · PIERRE BERTON

There are strange things done
in the midnight sun
By the men who moil for gold ...

up and cook imaginative meals, which he says is a throwback to his Boy Scout days, when he was designated camp cook.

Ted was awarded the Order of Canada in 1987 and was the first Canadian illustrator chosen by an international jury to be represented at the International Children's Book Exhibit in Bologna, Italy. He uses acrylic paint because it's clean and dries very quickly and sometimes he even uses a hair dryer to speed up the drying process and make corrections possible.

Ted's readers often ask him why he leaves out all the faces in his paintings, to which Ted replies that his reader's imaginations will put the features in for him. It's important to Ted to create books that will make his readers feel special. Encouraged himself as a child by a favourite teacher, Ted explains that his award-winning third book came as a result of his efforts to teach a class of grade two Cree children. Dissatisfied with the Dick and Jane books that were then the standard, Ted decided to write an illustrated book containing elements of the Cree culture, and the idea for *A Northern Alphabet* was born.

As a child, Ted was interested in reading tombstones. "My family were buried in the local churchyard. In England you could tell a

a northern alphabet

Ted Harrison

A Tundra Book

lot of history from a churchyard — plagues and things like that — and some of the epitaphs were very witty. And they're very quiet places, graveyards; you don't find a whole crowd there. I used to like to go and think."

When asked if he still seeks the quiet of a graveyard for peaceful reflection, Ted replies, "I'm living in Canada now. You can be alone in Canada quite easily." And judging by the great work he's done here, one would tend to agree that the great spaces of Canada are just the inspiration Ted Harrison needs.

"Think positive and have faith in your ability to succeed."

DO IT YOURSELF!

Ted Harrison draws his inspiration from the nature he sees around him. He suggests you do paintings, drawings, collages or models of the birds and animals in your neighbourhood. If you want, you could also draw some pet owners. Do any of them look like their pets?

Linda Hendry

🎨 *Illustrations only.*

Born:
August 5, 1961, in Nokomis, Saskatchewan

Home:
Toronto, Ontario

"**W**hen I was little, I thought it would be neat to be like Mr. Dress-Up; he was my inspiration," Linda Hendry says. "I'd see him on TV and I'd draw and make whatever he did. I thought it was a pretty cool career."

Now that she's an artist herself, Linda is convinced that she does indeed have a "pretty cool career." "What's most fun is when I draw something that makes me laugh; that's when I really like the job." Linda often hides things for her readers to find in her pictures. Look for secret notes written in the gravel in her illustrations.

Unlike many illustrators who work in stages, Linda Hendry always completes each illustration before moving on to the next one. "I start and finish, start and finish, start and finish — and maybe I shouldn't because sometimes the colours change. But when I start something, I like to get it done."

And just how *does* she get it done? Linda prepares rough linears, or sketches, of the book for her publisher to approve. These often go to the author for approval as well. Linda never works directly with the author when she works on a project. "In fact, sometimes I've never even met the author! We don't sit side by side at one desk."

THE CATS GET INTO THE ACT

When her roughs have been approved, Linda prefers to complete her illustrations with watercolours, because she says they're faster, neater and friendlier to the environment (no turpentine required!). "I use styrofoam meat trays to mix my colours on, then I can have one tray of greens for grasses and trees, one tray can be all blues and one can be all yellows." Linda laughs as she remembers a time when her cats decided to mix a few colours of their own, walking across the paint trays and her nearly finished artwork, leaving a trail of footprints behind them. She recalls, too, that she was able to turn the situation to her advantage by creating a dappled background for the illustration.

Linda tries to keep regular hours, working from about eight thirty in the morning to five at night, with breaks for her garden and the odd cup of tea. But she has had times when she's felt the need to paint at all hours. When she was working on *Malcolm's Runaway Soap*, for instance, she got up at three o'clock in the morning to change Malcolm's hair colour in all of the pictures.

"If something's very simple, I can do it in an hour and a half, two hours, but some pictures take two days. It depends really on how much detail is in the painting."

Projects that need more detail require Linda to take her sketchpad on the road or to think back to her own life experiences. *Malcolm's Runaway Soap* conjured memories of bath time when she was a child in Saskatchewan. There wasn't always a great deal of water available, and Linda's family used to share the same bath, taking turns, youngest to oldest.

Linda is just beginning work on her second project as a writer, and she really enjoys the freedom of doing both the illustrations and the

text. "In a way, it's because I don't have to do such tight linears. I go from a fairly loose rough, right to the page. That's partially because I'm working closely with the editor, but also because I don't feel like I have to show the author anything because I *am* the author."

When kids ask Linda which of her books is her favourite, she replies, "It always seems to be the one I'm working on at the time, because I always think I can do a better job. I'm always looking for something better and more fun."

"My parents wanted me to be a forest ranger or a veterinarian."

DO IT YOURSELF!

When Linda Hendry decides to do a book, it's usually because she has discovered something that she really likes drawing (as it was with junk for her book *Hilda Crumm's Hats*). Think about something you really like to draw and build a story around that.

Monica Hughes

Born:
November 3, 1925, in Liverpool, England

Home:
Edmonton, Alberta

Monica Hughes's favourite place to read when she was a child was at the top of the stairs beneath a skylight — "totally away from all adult interference and supervision." Her favourite authors were Arthur Ransom and E. Nesbit.

The decision to become a writer came early for Monica. "At the age of about ten, I decided I was going to be a novel writer when I grew up. I went out and spent all of my pocket money on a hard-backed blank book and I put an absolutely wonderful title on the front. Then I wrote 'Chapter One' inside and I waited for something to happen. It didn't." Monica says she used up several other manuscript books in this way, writing only titles and the words "Chapter One," before she finally managed to write her first stories.

Now, Monica finds ideas everywhere, and she writes them all down as soon as they come to her, before they vanish, keeping them in a file marked "Ideas." And any time she's stuck for something to write about, she'll go to that file and get them all out and think about them.

Ever since she received a CD player for Christmas, Monica has been listening to music while she writes. "I have found that working with music that has no interruptions — the radio doesn't work — is absolutely wonderful. If I'm writing a new book, I'll pick a piece of music that I think is going to be appropriate and that's what I play every single day."

Monica does a lot of research before she writes a book because she believes it's important to have what she calls "a really solid sense of place." In her book *The Crystal Drop*, which is set sometime in the next century in southern Alberta, Monica tells the story of a journey by two young people from the farm where they've been living to their uncle's place in the foothills. Before she began this story, Monica stayed in Lethbridge for a week. She visited Head-Smashed-In Buffalo Jump, and as she walked through the rooms of the museum she described what she saw while talking into a tape recorder. She also interviewed one of the archeologists while she was there. Then she drove along the back roads that her characters would have travelled, and noted the scenery and her car's odometer readings. Finally, she marked her characters' route on a big topographical map, then divided her book into chapters according to the distance the kids in her story would have been able to travel on foot.

After her research is finished, writing the first draft of a story isn't a long process for Monica. She writes between nine and twelve o'clock every morning, usually completing about two thousand words at each sitting to finish a chapter in two days.

If she isn't sure about spelling or punctuation, she doesn't worry about looking it up right away. Instead Monica marks it with a wiggly line and checks it later after she's finished her thought. When the first draft is complete, Monica puts her text into her computer and prints off a copy on which she uses a red pen to do her revisions. Monica then puts her manuscript aside for a time, so that when she reads it again she does so like a

> *"It doesn't do any good to hit the front of your head and say, Give me an idea!"*

stranger. It helps her to look at her work objectively.

When asked if she had any tips for young writers, Monica said, "Keep a journal." She reminds readers that a journal is not the same thing as a diary, where you're *forced* to put something down every day. A journal is a blank book where you put down your thoughts and your feelings. Says Monica, "It gets you in the habit of opening up." Monica also encourages kids to keep an ideas file and never give up!

DO IT YOURSELF!

Often, in Monica Hughes's books, characters with very different backgrounds share an adventure. She suggests that you and your friends clip a collection of human interest stories out of the newspaper. Then mix the clippings up, select two at random and write a story that ties the two together. Where the two ideas intersect, the story begins.

Bernice Thurman Hunter

Born:
November 3, 1922, in
Toronto, Ontario

Home:
Scarborough, Ontario

Bernice Thurman Hunter has always enjoyed reading realistic stories, so it follows that she would prefer writing realistic stories as well. But this particular kind of story requires a fair bit of research, so Bernice is always on the lookout for ideas.

"All of my books are based on real people. The Booky books are almost autobiographical — except that my brother says that that's not the way it happened. My family argues about that, and I just tell them to write their own book because I'm writing *my* memories."

Bernice remembers particularly fondly the time she had the honour of meeting one of her favourite authors. "I met L.M. Montgomery when I was fourteen years old — I idolized her, of course — and actually had tea with her in her back garden. I describe that event in *As Ever, Booky*; it's practically word for word what happened."

When she's not writing about her own life experiences, Bernice looks to other sources. One quest for a short story idea came to an end when she was standing in a department store line-up. "I heard these two women in front of me talking, so I just eavesdropped. They were talking about when they were kids; how they'd had this terrible fight and how they had resolved it. It was such a good idea that I just ran right home and wrote the story."

She also recalls with some embarrassment that, before she could escape, the little boy who was with the women turned around and said to his mother, "That nosy old lady's listening!" Bernice was caught in the act, but she was convinced it was worth it — and so was her publisher.

THE RISKS OF BEING A WRITER

In fact, Bernice learned from an early age that embarrassment isn't the only thing a writer is likely to suffer in search of a great story. When she was a girl, Bernice carefully put together her own newspaper. She made copies by hand, then passed them around the neighbourhood. "I thought I was a writer then."

But not everyone appreciated the effort that went into that first publication. Bernice recalls, "I remember I reported news on the kids and what they were up to. I had some boys beat me up after school because I put in some mischief they had gotten into!"

Years later, Bernice had a more positive newspaper experience; it was the first time she had ever published a piece for money. As a guest writer for *The Toronto Star*, Bernice wrote an article entitled "A Grandchild Can Make Life Beautiful Again" and received fifty dollars for her effort. Although she had published other articles, that first cheque made her feel like a real author. She fondly remembers receiving a letter from the paper's regular columnist, encouraging her to keep at it. "Seeing those words from another successful writer gave me the courage to keep on writing, which I did."

Over the years, Bernice's books have been appreciated by readers from eight to eighty. She recalls one particularly enthusiastic reader who sent her a list of her books,

beside which he had written how often he had reread each — some as many as ten or fifteen times!

Bernice welcomes the opportunity to motivate young readers. Every year she does a special Booky tour with a lucky group of schoolchildren in Scarborough, Ontario. After everyone is familiar with the Booky books, they board a bus and visit all of the places described in the series. Perhaps Bernice is thinking back to her own school days, when she herself was encouraged by a special grade eight teacher named Mr. Johnston. "He always liked my stories and because at that time I didn't have the nerve to stand up and talk in front of people — my legs would actually shake — he would read the stories to the class for me. That's what I call encouragement!"

"I like writing the type of stories that I like reading, which are real stories. I guess I'm just what you'd call a realist."

DO IT YOURSELF!

Bernice Thurman Hunter suggests you write about yourself. Think about an important or memorable thing that has happened to you, then start writing.

Dayal Kaur Khalsa

SELECTED TITLES

Born:
1943, in New York City, New York, USA

Died:
July 17, 1989

"I did not read anything except fairy tales and a series of travel books called *Children of Other Lands* until I was about thirteen years old," Dayal Kaur Khalsa once said. "The school called my mother in to discuss my 'problem.' She then handed me F. Scott Fitzgerald's *This Side of Paradise* — and I immediately became a rabid reader for life."

Dayal Kaur Khalsa was born in New York City, where she graduated from the City College of New York in liberal arts. As Dayal told an interviewer from The Canadian Children's Book Centre in 1988, "Right from the start I wanted to be an artist and a cowboy. Since I am a girl, I ended up being an artist. But — the nice thing about being an artist is that I am now writing and illustrating a book about how I wanted to be a cowboy and what things I would have done."

Dayal found her start in publishing when May Cutler, publisher at Tundra Books, saw some of her drawings and asked whether Dayal would consider doing a series for babies. Dayal, who was very fond of babies, agreed and the BAABEE series was born.

LOOKING FOR ADVENTURE

From there, Dayal went on to write about other things that were dear to her. "When I was a young teenager, and wanted to be a writer, and couldn't wait to leave home and go on the road in search of adventure to write about, my mother said, 'There are stories right in your own back yard.' 'Hah!' I said. So I left home, went on the road, had lots of adventures, and eventually, twenty-five years later, the first book I published took place in my backyard of childhood. Hah!"

HOW **PIZZA** CAME TO OUR TOWN

BY DAYAL KAUR KHALSA

In fact, true to her mother's words, most of Dayal's books ended up being based on things she had experienced as a child. Her book *I Want a Dog* came about as Dayal remembered her own longing for a dog when she was young, and although her young heroine finally achieves her goal through determination and creativity, Dayal recalled that she was not so lucky. "Of course it's an inspiring lie," she confessed in 1987. "When I was a child, I always wanted two dogs I could name Ginger and Pedro. It was my dream in life. When I was thirty-one, I finally got a dog. It was the size of seven beagles, and had already been named Julian."

After deciding what kind of book she wanted to make, Dayal would start by completing all of the illustrations in an opaque kind of watercolour paint called gouache. Only then would she begin to write the story on her word processor.

With strains of bluegrass, Beethoven or Bach to inspire her, Dayal would begin sketches for her picture books, all the while sneaking in bits and pieces of famous paintings to surprise her readers, providing them not only with delightful stories, but also with a rousing game of "find the hidden painting." Look for Seurat's painting "Sunday Afternoon on the

Island of La Grande Jatte" in *I Want a Dog* and Tom Thomson's "The West Wind" in *Julian*.

Dayal Kaur Khalsa always managed to find the positive side of things, and her determination as a writer and as an illustrator enabled her to publish seven of her eight books while enduring painful cancer treatments. Shortly after Dayal's death, May Cutler, her publisher, praised her as: "…that rarest and most precious of individuals in the children's book world. She would bring in her latest illustrations and tell us the story with obvious delight. One sensed how much pleasure she had working them out."

> *"My advice to children who want to write is to write down everything that pops into their heads, and keep an idea book."*

DO IT YOURSELF!

Dayal Kaur Khalsa always enjoyed surprising her readers with the little touches she added to her illustrations. Why not try this yourself? Draw a picture of something ordinary, then add small out-of-place details to surprise your friends. For example, if you were drawing a Canadian forest, you could sneak one tiny palm tree into the illustration.

Gordon Korman

SELECTED TITLES

This Can't Be Happening at Macdonald Hall
1978

Bugs Potter Live at Nickaninny
1983

No Coins, Please
1984

The Zucchini Warriors
1988

Radio Fifth Grade
1989

Losing Joe's Place
(American Library Association Best Book Award for Young Adults)
1990

Macdonald Hall Goes Hollywood
1991

The Twinkie Squad
1992

The Toilet Paper Tigers
1993

Why Did the Underwear Cross the Road?
1994

Born:
October 23, 1963, in Montreal, Quebec

Home:
New York City, New York, USA

Toronto, Ontario

Pompano Beach, Florida, USA

Almost everyone has heard about Gordon Korman's surprise seventh grade leap into publishing, but for those of you who haven't: "I'm running around to schools apologizing for the seventh grade story, but the fact is I can't leave it out. I feel a little bit like Mick Jagger who said there was no way that he was going to be singing 'Satisfaction' at forty, and he's fifty and still singing the same song. I'm thirty and still talking about seventh grade. But basically what happened was we had four months to work on the same project and I wrote *This Can't Be Happening at Macdonald Hall*. At the time I was the class monitor for Arrow and TAB book clubs, so I felt this corpo-

rate responsibility towards Scholastic — although strangely they didn't know about me! I sent it in to the address on the book club sheet and I guess it went to an editor. I got really lucky. I think there was a lot of right place and right time involved."

The publishing process was not all glamour for Gordon when his first book was published. "I was thrilled with the way it came out. But you have to remember what it's like to be a preteen. From the day I signed that contract to the day it came out we're looking at close to a year and a half. I expect it to take that long now, but that was forever for me then. By the time the book came out I was practically sick of it."

Even today, Gordon admits that he's usually tired of each new book as it's finished. "I certainly have read it upside down and underwater a million times by the time it comes out. I think the difference now is that I've always got something else going. I'm always writing a new book while the one prior to it is going through editing, and the one before that is in galleys. I always have a number of things happening, so I'm never really conscious of the wait like I was before."

CRAZY HOURS

When he was first starting out, Gordon spent a great deal of time on his writing. "When I was fourteen and fifteen writing some of those older books like *Go Jump in the Pool* and *Beware the Fish*, I would say I did the bulk of my best work in the middle of the night. I wouldn't start until eleven and worked through till three a.m." Gordon says he kept these crazy hours only in the summertime, which is when he did most of his writing while he was still in school. Nowadays he does far more work during the day and in the evenings.

Life experiences do find their way into Gordon's writing, but they are never the main story line. "They're more support stuff. The school in *Son of Interflux* was an arts high school, and I wrote it while I was in the school of the arts in NYU. I took the college kids I knew and scaled them down four years to be in high school and wrote about my friends."

Gordon's latest book was also inspired by something that happened in his own life. "*The Toilet Paper Tigers* is about baseball and the idea started when I'd written

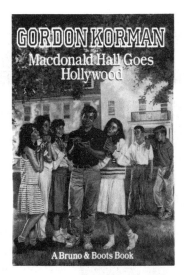

about hockey in the Bruno and Boots books and I'd written about football in *Zucchini Warriors* and my friends were saying 'When are you going to write a baseball book?' I really didn't want to write one, so to shut them up I said 'Tell you what, if the Blue Jays ever win the World Series, I'll write a baseball book.' I didn't think they were actually going to do it — let alone twice!"

Gordon loves his work as a writer, but he also loves the opportunities for travel that his writing affords him. "I've had a chance to go to eight provinces, forty-five states, six European countries, and this year I'm going to the Far East. So I've really had a chance to log some miles — and the Frequent Flyer bonus points haven't been too bad either! I really enjoy seeing other places and getting around. On the other hand, sometimes that's a negative part because it doesn't give you a whole lot of continuity to your life when you're moving around so much."

Everywhere Gordon goes, he collects remarkable and surprising pieces of information. For example, at one school he visited in his travels, a student assured him that it is indeed possible to suck M&M's through a tuba — a tidbit that found its way into one of Gordon's books. "I never run out of ideas completely. I always have a lot of things in my mind, so it's really more a question of picking which one to write about."

"When you're writing, you're always rewriting."

DO IT YOURSELF!

Gordon Korman says that the most fun he had writing *The Toilet Paper Tigers* was inventing wacky baseball players. Create a team to play your favourite sport. Who are the stars? the duds? the crazy personalities? How far can they go? All the way to the championships?

Maryann Kovalski

SELECTED TITLES

Brenda and Edward
1984

The Wheels on the Bus
1987

Jingle Bells
1988

 Alice and the Birthday Giant
1989

 Grandma's Secret
1989

Frank and Zelda
1990

 Junk-Pile Jennifer
1991

 The Big Storm
1992

Take Me Out to the Ball Game
1992

 Doctor Knickerbocker and Other Rhymes
1993

 I Went to the Zoo
1993

 Illustrations only.

Born:
June 4, 1951, in New York City, New York, USA

Home:
Toronto, Ontario

Maryann Kovalski grew up in New York City, where she remembers spending one special evening alone at the library, gazing at the pages of a Babar book. "Being from the Bronx you couldn't get a place more exotic than the south of France. I was completely absorbed in the book and when I looked up I realized it was nightfall. Now, I have three brothers — who had obviously been looking for me in the street — and I remember going home and seeing each of them come running towards me saying, 'You're in trouble!'" That's the danger of reading!

Even though she was an insatiable reader, Maryann always knew she wanted to be an artist. Although she confesses that for a time she didn't know exactly what an illustrator was. "In my high school we would just take old pictures and copy them, so I didn't really know about any practical way that art could be applied."

When she attended art school, Maryann soon learned that illustrators were the people who drew the pictures for magazines, newspapers and picture books. Soon after graduation, she moved to Canada and was approached by Kids Can Press to do her first book for kids. After that, there was no stopping her.

"I find I can really go full steam ahead on illustrations. I sit down and get cracking right away. It's something I can do for six hours straight." Writing, however, is considerably harder for her.

"When I'm getting stuck I find it's best to just write. Just write anything. Write badly. People who don't succeed at things are usually the people who stop when they're in the doing-it-badly stage. They're not going to push through that great mountain of bad work to get the little spoonful of good work which is waiting for them on the other side.

"I also keep a journal. I try to write every day and sometimes I even write ten pages. They might be reminiscences; they might be things that are happening in my life; or sometimes I might be working out a problem."

KEEP YOUR EYES OPEN

When Maryann needs ideas for her paintings, she believes that walking and looking are very important. "I used to run off to the library's picture collection to find

out things like what a building looked like, but with *The Wheels on the Bus*, I found that just standing on a street corner helped me get that feeling of a winter evening at five-thirty, when lots of people are rushing around and there's a carnival-like colour to the lights. I just kept looking and looking and it all went into my head and into my hand, then out onto the paper."

Maryann confesses that it's sometimes hard for her to agree on the revisions her editor suggests. "Occasionally, I have moments where I say, This is good. But a lot of times you don't know what's going to work until the book's been published and reviewed. Then six months later you pick it up and say, That was pretty good, or, Ooh, that really didn't work."

To help her through the tough revision process, Maryann uses what she calls the "three times rule." "If you're showing something

"You have to do something badly before you're going to do it well."

to someone and they make a criticism or they're confused about something and it comes up three times, you know that something's not working."

Maryann tells children not to worry so much about being professionals. "Savour this time of your life when you can draw what you

like when you like, and don't worry so much about getting praise or criticism. I think that's really important because when you hope for recognition, you second guess yourself and it takes away from the sheer pleasure of it."

Paul Kropp

Born:
February 22, 1948, in Buffalo, New York, USA

Home:
Toronto, Ontario

Paul Kropp made his career choice when he was still a kid. "For many years, I wanted to be a fireman, of course, and then, under the influence of two early television shows, *Perry Mason* and *The Defenders*, I decided to become a lawyer. Had I been smart I would have stayed with that, because almost all of my friends have become lawyers and they're much wealthier than I am. But I decided to become a writer in grade six, thanks to my principal, a fellow named Alfred J. Labiak who was the subject of a feature piece in the first underground newspaper to be produced at Public School 81. The underground newspaper was produced on my typewriter because I was the one who had a typewriter.

"Mr. Labiak had the paper in his hands within three days and called me into the office and said: Kropp did you do this? I said yes and I was punished. That was when I learned that writing has power."

Paul Kropp was teaching at a vocational school when he decided to write his first novel. He wanted to write something for the kids who didn't enjoy reading, and put together the first few pages of what eventually became *Burn Out*. Then, he went looking for publishers. "I went alphabetically, starting with the A's. I got as far as the C's." After Collier Macmillan agreed to sign him up, Paul says, "I was so thrilled I almost forgot to ask them to pay me anything."

IDEAS FROM REAL LIFE

Paul always gets his ideas from real life. He explains, "I have a limited imagination. I almost

invariably draw characters from either a school that I visit or a school where I teach."

Although his writing no longer permits him to teach full time, Paul continues to teach a creative writing course at the high school level. He says it helps him to stay current and, of course, allows him to find models for the characters in his books.

He also finds that because his students are comfortable working with him, they aren't afraid to tell him what they think about his books. "My creative writing class felt no bones about saying: Boy, why don't you cut the first page of this new book of yours and start with page two? And I imagine they were right. I've done that, anyhow, so I hope they're right!"

In addition to working directly with the students who will eventually be reading his books, Paul prepares in other ways. "My work requires a great deal of research. I've never been in a gang. I've never smoked dope. I've never been a woman. I've never been on a horse. I've never ridden a motorcycle. I've never been in a burning building. My life has been remarkably dull and almost everything I write requires a fair deal of slug labour to find out how things really go. Of my life, all I can reveal is that I play a fair deal of croquet, and since I've never been able to write a book about croquet, everything else has had to be researched."

For his book *Wild One*, Paul Kropp had to go out and take a good look at a horse. "I've always quite despised horses — and I say that straightforwardly — and after I had finished the book I despised them even more. I think they smell bad and they're quite dangerous and they can hit you with their hooves and

do nasty things. I never once, while writing the book, got on a horse.

"So it's possible, I think, through talking to people who have actually lived the experience, to get what I think is a very effective way of presenting it to others. The experience of a flat track bike racer, for instance, who has done it for twenty years, is very different from my experience getting on the thing for the first time."

Paul is continually fiddling with his manuscripts, taking long showers to organize his thoughts. "I'm very scared when I let go of the manuscript at the last moment that there will be something that I should have fixed, but the nature of writing a novel is that you keep on working at it until they decide to put it in print."

And that's exactly what he does.

"If you haven't read two thousand books by the time you're twenty, you haven't read enough."

DO IT YOURSELF!

Take a tip from Paul Kropp and do some research on something you know nothing about, then include it in a piece of writing. Interview someone at a police station to find out more about police procedures; call a factory and ask for a tour of the assembly line; or contact a worker in a fast food restaurant and ask to see what they do on an average day. The more you learn, the more interesting your writing will be.

Michael Arvaarluk Kusugak

SELECTED TITLES

A Promise Is a Promise
(co-author)
1988

Baseball Bats for Christmas
1990

Hide and Sneak
1992

Northern Lights: The Soccer Trails
(Ruth Schwartz Children's Book Award)
1993

Born:
April 27, 1948, in Cape Fullerton, N.W.T.

Home:
Rankin Inlet, N.W.T.

"**W**e only spoke Inuktitut when I was little, and there weren't books written in Inuktitut except the Roman Catholic prayer book that we used, so we didn't read a lot," Michael Arvaarluk Kusugak recalls. "What we got more of was storytelling. Storytelling has always been a great tradition with the Inuit. There are legends that have been told from generation to generation for hundreds of years. I grew up in a tiny community called Repulse Bay, where I spent a lot of time at my grandmother's hut. And I think it was from her that I first heard the stories."

After growing up in that close community where stories were told, but rarely read, Michael had to go away to study. "I really didn't read until I started going to school. The very first books that we had were

the school readers called *Fun with Dick and Jane*. They were just hideous things and I don't think anybody ever fell in love with those.

"I went to school in a lot of different places. I had to leave my parents and my community. And I had to go to places away from my people. I went to Yellowknife where there are trees and where — at that time — there were no Inuit. Then I had to go to Churchill, Manitoba and I graduated from high school in Saskatoon, Saskatchewan. It was very hard to develop a group of friends. It was so much easier just to sit and write something."

MICHAEL MEETS MUNSCH

In this way, Michael began to develop his skills as a writer, but it wasn't for many years that he finally considered doing it for a living. "I was working for the government of the Northwest Territories and I had been working for the government for a long time. I had this idea that it was going to be a career until I retired, but I didn't really enjoy it all that much. I joined the library board in Rankin Inlet and one day when we had a meeting we invited Robert Munsch. He came and he stayed with us and I started telling stories. One day, he said, 'Why don't you write them down?' And, as they say, the rest is history."

"History," as Michael calls it, began when he submitted his first story to Annick Press and it was rejected. "It was the most humiliating experience I've ever had, I think. But at the same time, I would imagine that a lot of people get discouraged by that kind of treatment from a publisher, and probably in a lot of cases it's just as well. Because unless you're willing to persevere, and keep going after different publishers, I don't think there's any sense in going on."

Now, for all you readers who write and ask Michael: How big is an igloo? here's his answer. "We build three different sizes of igloos. One is for when you go out hunting and you build an igloo that is just big enough for you and your companion — it's like a pup tent; it's small and easy to build and it heats up quickly so you don't freeze to death. The second kind is a live-in igloo, which would be big enough for your whole family and it would have a sleeping platform, a bit of a floor and a cooking counter. The third kind is a huge, huge igloo that we build to hold parties in. It's called a qaggi."

Michael does *not* work in an igloo. "I have an office which is right next door to my house. It's a big shed and it's very quiet. Every morning at six-thirty I get up and I start a pot of coffee. Then I come over here, start up my wood stove and I start to work."

Michael writes his stories in English and not in his native Inuktitut. "I made this decision when I decided to become a writer, because I think you have to write for your audience and the Inuktitut audience is really small — even the Canadian audience is not that big!

"The actual writing part doesn't take all that long. It might take a week or two weeks. Then, after it's done the real work starts. The 'real work' is rewriting over and over and over again until it sounds good — until it sounds like somebody has been telling the story for hundreds of years."

"Grandmother, please tell me a story."

DO IT YOURSELF!

Michael Kusugak is currently working on a new story about an airship that flew over Repulse Bay when he was a boy. At the time, his whole community was very afraid because they had never seen anything like it. Michael suggests that you try writing about an historical event from the perspective of someone who witnessed it happening.

Kim LaFave

Born:
January 12, 1955, in
Vancouver, British Columbia

Home:
Roberts Creek, British
Columbia

"**I**'m the youngest in the family, and when everyone would head off to school, I'd just break out pencils and paper and start drawing," Kim LaFave remembers. "That was my company and my entertainment."

Kim studied commercial art and went on to do illustrations for magazines. But when he was introduced to children's publishing, he found things in the work that he hadn't before. "You had a chance to get a lot more deeply involved in something. The other jobs came in and out pretty quickly, but these ones you had a long time to think about. You had the opportunity to work with interesting people and then, when the book was done, it sort of took on a life of its own."

Now, as it is with most children's book illustrators, Kim receives manuscripts from his publisher and has the opportunity to decide which he'd like to work on. How does he know which to choose? "You receive a lot of manuscripts and if they don't excite you, then you just don't take them on. But every once in a while one comes along and you just feel very close to the character. I think that's because when I draw, I draw from my imagination and I draw from my experience."

THE YOUNGEST IN THE FAMILY

Such a book is Kim's new project, Sheree Fitch's *I Am Small*. "It's easy to illustrate a book like that because I was the youngest in the family and I remember being small very, very clearly. I remember everybody's shoes being so much bigger than mine — all those kinds of things that she talks about in the story."

Kim gets up in the morning and starts working almost immediately, because he solves a lot of his illustration problems when he's asleep. He treats each book as if it were one great big illustration.

"I start out with little tiny sketches and scribble them all up really quick, so the first time I do the sketches for a story I may only spend an hour on it." Kim then does detailed final drawings in pencil. "I'm always going back and forth as I go along. It's the same with the finished art, because in the months and months it can take to do the paintings for a book, a lot can happen: the light changes; I start running out of paint so I start using different colours. I want the things that need to be consistent, to *be* consistent — like the colours, costumes and skin tones — so I'll go through and do all the backgrounds at once, then all the foregrounds, then all the characters. Just so that those things remain consistent."

For Kim, this back-and-forth technique has another advantage. "It gives you that chance for ideas to develop. If you start one and take it right to finish, then you're kind of committed and you have to do all the rest the same way. Then you know what it's going to turn out like and *then* it becomes boring because you know you've got about twenty illustrations you have to

"It was interesting, and I got to work with some great people."

make look just like the first one."

Kim notes: "When kids are really young they're just naturals — they draw and they're totally accepting of everything they do. Then, as they get older they start to want to draw more perfectly and they become much more self-conscious and self-aware. The big thing I've found working myself is to keep an open mind, because all those things you start calling mistakes, sometimes are the the best parts of a painting."

DO IT YOURSELF!

Here's a tip from Kim LaFave: the next time you're painting a picture and something doesn't come out exactly the way you expected, don't panic. Take a moment to really look at what you've done before throwing everything away. It may be that a slip of the brush is the best thing that ever happened to your painting!

Dennis Lee

Born:
August 31, 1939, in Toronto,
Ontario
Home:
Toronto, Ontario

The first time Dennis Lee ever saw his work in print was in a children's magazine called *Wee Wisdom* when he was only nine years old. "I sent in a poem called 'If' which appeared there, and I was so staggered by the Nobel-Prize-winning feel of my achievement that I didn't publish another poem for thirteen years," says Dennis with a laugh.

Dennis Lee is now an experienced poet for children and for adults. He explains that he came up with the idea for what is probably his best-known poem, "Alligator Pie," in a rather unusual way. He had been writing Mother Goose-type rhymes for his own kids, and was on his way to do an errand when it came to him.

"I got on my bike and I had a shopping bag or something slung over my shoulder. I headed off, and as my feet were going round on the pedals the words started coming into my brain: 'Alligator pie, alligator pie…' to the rhythm of my feet going round. It seemed so airhead that I tried to dismiss it, but it kept coming: 'Alligator pie, alligator pie. If I don't get some I think I'm gonna die.' Finally the thing was bugging me so much, I stopped the bike, turned it around, went back to the house, got a piece of paper and scribbled down however much had come, thinking that that would exorcise it and it wouldn't bother me any more." But, of course, that was just the beginning for Dennis and for "Alligator Pie." Dennis jokes, "It actually became a complete alligator around my neck!"

The collection of poems that eventually became the manuscript for *Alligator Pie* took Dennis over nine years to complete. Dennis met with the publisher at Macmillan, who had some very special testing in mind. Dennis says, "He went out into his neighbourhood, rounded up a batch of kids and said, 'Come on, we're going to sit down and read some poems.' He dragged them into his living room and he sat and read to them from the manuscript. Of course, there were no pictures or anything like that to hold their interest, but he was satisfied that they were enjoying it, so he got back to me and said, 'We're very interested.'"

ONE BOOK BECOMES TWO

As it turned out, nine years of work had actually produced enough material for two books. Dennis and his publisher decided to split the material in half, creating a book for young children, which would be *Alligator Pie*, and another for older readers, called *Nicholas Knock and Other People*.

Dennis had intended to title his book *Dance across the Earth*, after one of the poems in his collection. But this changed when his publisher joined him at some of his school readings. Dennis explains, "He noticed at the end of every one that the kids would come out chanting 'Alligator Pie' to each other, which was just one of thirty or forty poems I might do with them while I was in there, and eventually he said, 'You know, I think you'd better

just accept the inevitable. The kids are naming your book for themselves.'" And so it was that *Alligator Pie* found a name.

Although it no longer takes Dennis nine years to write a book, he frequently does as many as fifty drafts of a poem. He likens his writing style to that of many sculptors who sense that the form they hope to carve is already in the stone, believing all that must be done is to chip away everything that *isn't* the sculpture. "I get that sense with writing. Of course, I have to generate the stone in terms of endless drafts in the process, but then I give things permission not to be in the poem, so that the actual poem itself can stand out."

When kids ask Dennis where he gets his ideas, he jokes about ordering them like pizzas, then more seriously explains that, for him, writing depends a great deal on intuition. "Even young children know about intuition — know about discovering things that they know without knowing *why* they know them."

He then goes on to ask them: How does your body know how to move when you play a sport? How do you know what you want to include next when you're doing a drawing? In a way, it just happens.

"I live in Toronto and down on Spadina Avenue there's a twenty-four-hour place that you can call up and say I'd like one idea, fourteen inches. I need double peppers, double cheese and pepperoni on it."

DO IT YOURSELF!

Dennis Lee enjoys writing poems that rhyme, and free verse poems, too. Write a poem that rhymes, then take the same basic idea and write a poem in free verse.

Michèle Lemieux

SELECTED TITLES

La baleine fantastique
1980

What's that Noise?
1984

 Lucky Hans
1985

 Winter Magic
1985

 Amahl and the Night Visitors
1986

 A Gift from Saint Francis
1989

 Voices on the Wind: Poems for all Seasons
1990

Peter and the Wolf
1991

The Pied Piper of Hamlin
1993

 There Was an Old Man: A Gallery of Nonsense Rhymes
1994

 Illustrations only.

Born:
May 29, 1955, in Quebec City, Quebec

Home:
Montreal, Quebec

Michèle Lemieux became enchanted with the arts at a very early age. "I spent most of my free time as a child doing crafts and art. I did a lot of puppets; I wrote fairy tales and puppet shows. I had a very good friend who liked doing things like that, and together we did lots of things involving music, writing and drawing.

"Once in school we had an oral assignment where we had to say in front of the class what we would like to do when we grew up. I took this question very seriously and I remember I felt so terrible because I said I wanted to write books and make pictures inside of them. Everyone else said they wanted to be nurses or teachers or mothers and I thought: Oh no, I'm all wrong!"

Years later, when she began working as a professional illustra-tor, Michèle still felt alone in her desire to publish books for children. "There weren't many children's books being done here in Quebec and I had the feeling that what I wanted to do was not something I could do here. I worked as an illustrator for advertising and I hated it. It was so bad I was looking in the Yellow Pages for another profession. So I decided to go to Europe and try something else. I went to Germany for what I thought would be a couple of months and I stayed for five years. That's where I had my real start." Even now that she's back in Canada, Michèle still tries to get to the European book fairs every year to keep herself motivated.

Inspiration is easy to find for Michèle. "Ideas are everywhere, you just have to notice them. Sit in a bus on a boring day and look at the people. You'll get plenty of ideas. A woman's nose may be amazing or the feet of a man sitting next to you may be huge. Very often, I sit on the bus and I try to guess who will come in next. They're all different and they all have different faces and this is a source of inspiration for me. Just look at what is going on around you. Take it and put it in another context — then it becomes magic."

A TRICKY QUESTION

When kids ask Michèle how long it takes to do each picture, she explains that this is a tricky question to answer. "I like to change the medium when I work and it certainly makes a big difference in the time I spend on a picture. Also, some pictures seem very simple, but I may have to redo them five or six times before I'm happy with them. Say the last picture I do is the one I pick, and it took me three hours. But it's the fifth time I did it, so it actually took me a week."

"When I work, if I'm too stiff or I'm not concentrating or I'm just not achieving what I want, very often I just stop and paint anything that comes into my head. Then I go back to the picture and it goes much better." This technique, Michèle admits, may also extend the time it takes to complete an illustration.

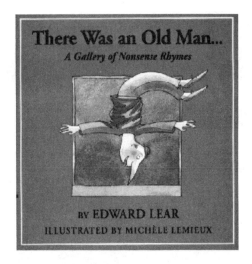

When she has time from her work as an illustrator and a teacher at L'université du Québec à Montréal, Michèle enjoys visiting kids in schools. Often, at the end of her visit, she'll do an original drawing for the class. On a huge piece of paper, she'll draw a simple character, then she'll ask the class ques-

tions about her picture, drawing what the kids ask her to draw. For instance, a picture which begins as a plain little pig could end up being a granny pig going to the park with her grandson, or it could be a punk pig on his way to rob a bank. It always turns out differently. And it always gives her a good idea about what kids like.

Back when she was first starting out and feeling discouraged, Michèle remembered how much she loved what she was doing and resolved to continue, saying, "I want to keep going until someone can prove to me that what I do is bad and ugly and stupid and children hate it." Needless to say, this has never happened. And we're all very glad about that.

"I spend a lot of time questioning myself."

DO IT YOURSELF!

Michèle Lemieux suggests you make one list of objects and a second of animals. Then choose one thing from each list and combine drawings of both to create one creature. Can you imagine, for example, what a hat and a rabbit would look like if they were drawn as one creature? What about a horse and a bench?

Jean Little

Born:
January 2, 1932, in Taiwan
Home:
Guelph, Ontario

"**A**ll my family inspired me to be interested in books," Jean Little recalls. "Then out of the interest in books came the interest in writing."

And so Jean chose her profession accordingly. "I always wanted to write, but I was going to *teach* to make a living — people had told me for years you couldn't make a living as a writer." But that hasn't turned out to be true for Jean. In fact, not long after she published her first books, she gave up teaching full time to take up a career in writing — although she still works with kids and writers in classroom settings.

Jean describes her first publishing experience as marvellous. "I finished the book to the best of my ability — I had a lot of fun writing it — and sent it in to a competition, and won. Right away I got a thou-sand dollar publisher's prize which was an advance on royalties, and the story was published. I remember the editor coming up from Boston to take me out to lunch and that was extremely exciting."

CREATING REAL CHARACTERS

When kids ask Jean if her characters are based on real people, Jean replies, "They're usually more real to me than the children who ask the question are, because they have a long life that no living child will have. Anna [in her book *From Anna*] will always be nine, even though in another book she's fourteen. Because you can always open up the book and she's nine again, and she'll do that forever as long as there is a book."

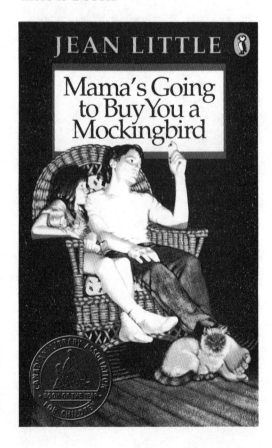

Jean goes on to say, "My characters are real enough that if I get halfway through writing a book and decide I don't want to finish it, what makes me finish it is the characters. Because if I don't finish it, it's like killing them. Their only chance to live is if I finish the book."

Another reason Jean Little's characters are so real to her is that they're largely based on her memories. Just read her autobiographical books, *Little by Little* and *Stars Come Out Within*, and you'll see that many characters and events from her own childhood have crept into her stories.

Jean says that she wrote these books about her childhood because she was always having to complete the biographical questionnaires her publishers sent her. "I hate filling out forms. My life sounds so devoid of interest. It seems like all I've done is go to school and write books. It seems so deadly dull and yet it isn't really like that at all."

Does Jean write from an outline? "Never! In my head I sort of know what's coming, but one of the things that keeps me writing — and this is for sure — is the delight of

"My family were all readers. We read aloud and read together and read separately."

discovering stuff. I like not knowing what's going to happen at any given moment. It's like working on a puzzle, except that you're far more emotionally involved."

When Jean can't find information to describe something in her books, she finds a way of getting around it. "Years ago, Lorrie McLaughlin told me that there was a sea battle in one of her books and she didn't know what the ships looked like, so she put the kid up a tree where he could hear the battle — because she knew how it would sound — but where he couldn't see anything because of the leaves. If the research isn't pertinent to the plot you don't need to do it. You *can* avoid it."

And what is Jean's advice for kids who want to become writers? "Write on Saturdays. Don't just write when a teacher says: Now it's time for writing. If you want to write, you have to be able to motivate yourself. Starting is half the battle. One way to do that is to write on holidays, write on Saturdays and write on your own time, so you can learn how to make yourself get going and do it."

DO IT YOURSELF!

Choose a minor character from a favourite story and write a diary for that character. In the beginning, you'll probably end up writing about things that actually happen in the book, but eventually you may think of other things to write about and you'll begin to see your character as a whole, real person. Ask Jean Little and she'll tell you that's exactly what happens when you're writing.

Janet Lunn

Born:
December 28, 1928, in Dallas, Texas, USA

Home:
Hillier, Ontario

Janet Lunn's first job was in a local public library in Rye, New York where she grew up and where she's sure that even today she'd be able to find the collection of E. Nesbit books she so loved as a child. Her all time favourite, however, was *The Secret Garden* by Frances Hodgson Burnett. "I read it still about once a year!"

Part of the reason young readers today are as entranced by Janet's books as she was by those of her childhood is her ability to transport her readers to another place and time. "As a writer of historical fiction, a lot of time is spent researching. I don't want to write about a place that my feet haven't been. If I'm going to take you to the north of Scotland, I've got to have been there so I know what it feels like. And then, of course, there's reading

the history of the time, reading about the music, the costume. There's a lot of stuff to look up, but I *always* travel to the places that I'm writing about."

Janet doesn't decide to write stories about places she'd like to visit, though; in fact she never knows where she's going to have to go until the idea for a story comes to her. And that idea can come from absolutely anywhere. "*The Root Cellar* is about my own house where I do have a ghost, and *Amos's Sweater* is very definitely about a sheep that I met.

"I have ideas backed up like people trying to get into a fast food restaurant. Those are the ones I think I'll write next, but then some other idea marches right up to the front of the line and pushes everybody else out."

When Janet has decided on one idea she isn't always eager to begin. "The part that frightens me is actually plunging into a new book. I'm so scared of it. I know that when I start writing I'm going to be lost in that world for two, three, four years, and so I shy away from it."

But when Janet does get going, there's almost no stopping her. Even when she's finished she can't help making endless adjustments. "I like rewriting — obviously, or I wouldn't do it so much — some people just hate it, but not me." Janet's love of editing is so great that she admits she could easily be editing forever, and recalls a favourite story about a famous French painter who, when he was a very old man, would go the Louvre and touch up his paintings while his friends kept the guards busy. Janet agrees that it's harder to fiddle with a book once it's printed, but she does make small changes when she reads her work out loud to students.

In fact, reading aloud is a big part of Janet's revision process. "When you read something out loud to yourself, you don't hear the flaws the way you do when you read it to an audience. It doesn't require that a person tell you all the things they think are right and wrong; it's just that your antennae are much more out there when you've got someone listening to you."

For Janet Lunn, the only thing as hard as starting a book is finishing it. "I mourn a book that's finished — not the history — but the fiction that I really get involved in. I mourn that when it's over. You live with these people a long time, and closely. I still remember the day I called the publisher to see if the book *The Root Cellar* was ready. She said, 'Yup, they're here, you can come and get yours,' and I sat down and cried because I knew it *really* was over."

Janet says this mourning is similar to the feeling you get when you come to the end of a great book and realize that you have to let those characters go "except that instead of having had one reading experience, you've lived with these people for a couple of years. And suddenly it's over. You realize you can go and visit, but it's not the same."

But like her troubles with getting started, Janet has found ways of getting over her mourning at the end of a project. "Then, of course, I'm fickle and the next thing I know I'm into a new one."

"I probably made the decision to become a writer around the time I decided to have feet."

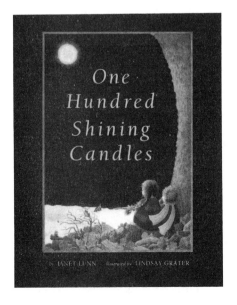

One Hundred Shining Candles

by JANET LUNN   illustrated by LINDSAY GRATER

DO IT YOURSELF!

Janet Lunn believes that in order to train yourself as a writer, you have to have eyes like a painter's eyes: you need to look at things and be able to describe them. If you're really serious about writing, every day describe something new. Use the best few words you can find in your description.

Claire Mackay

SELECTED TITLES

Mini-Bike Hero
1974

Mini-Bike Racer
1975

Exit Barney McGee
1979

**One Proud Summer
(co-author)**
*(Ruth Schwartz Children's
Book Award)*
1981

Mini-Bike Rescue
1982

The Minerva Program
1984

**Pay Cheques and Picket
Lines: All About Unions
in Canada**
1987

The Toronto Story
1990

Touching All the Bases
1994

**Bats About Baseball
(co-author)**
1994

*Vicky Metcalf Award winner,
1983*

Born:
December 21, 1930, in
Toronto, Ontario

Home:
Toronto, Ontario

"**I** always had it in the back of
my mind from a very early
age that I would write; although I'm
not sure that I said to myself, I
think I will be an author," Claire
Mackay says. "I loved words and I
loved putting them together. I even
did it when I didn't have to. I think
that's probably a tip-off — that you
eventually make your way to your
proper vocation."

On her way, Claire remembers
the encouraging words of a teacher.
"In high school I had an absolutely
marvellous English teacher in
grades twelve and thirteen. He actually suggested that I could be a journalist and I just about fell down
and licked his shoes at that point. I
did try in college. I went and
applied at the college paper, but my
first story for *The Varsity* just didn't
cut it — that was my first and last

story. It was so full of flowery
description that they felt my talents
didn't quite match their needs."

Despite this first job — or perhaps because of it — Claire put off a
serious attempt at writing for a long
time. This, she says, was at least
partly because there were no role
models around — at least not like
there are today, as Claire and other
notable writers visit classrooms
across the country.

IN SEARCH OF A ROLE MODEL

"Nobody came to our school and
said, I write books. So I had this
vision — which was highly roman-
ticized, I'm sure — of some distant
person in an English castle writing
books. That was one of the reasons
that I neglected to apply myself to
what I should have been doing all
my life. The other reason was that I
was very fearful. I had read so much

good stuff that I had somehow achieved the notion that I could never be very good — that if I couldn't be excellent, then why try — which is a really self-defeating way to go about your life. Nevertheless, I was afraid that I would just make a hash of it, so I delayed trying it until close to middle age."

Claire rediscovered her desire to write when, as an adult student, another teacher suggested she give creative writing a try. She found she was better suited to writing fiction than she was to newspaper work, and when her first book, *Mini-Bike Hero*, was submitted to her publisher, it was accepted at once. "No one was more astonished than I, and I haven't had any problems since. It just turned my life completely around."

In fact, the biggest surprise for Claire was the fact that everyone began calling her a writer. "I had some notion that nobody would notice that this book had been written, and that I had written it — although I don't know *how* I thought I could be anonymous because the first printing sold out in about four months. All of a sudden people were calling me a writer; I personally could not apply that noun to myself for the first four books. I used to whisper it. People would ask me what I do and I'd say: Oh, I'm a writer."

Claire is embarrassed to admit that she works better if someone is hanging over her saying: Get that done. And she confesses to being a terrible procrastinator. She reads mystery stories and makes lists to waste time, but she has one truly unusual habit, too. "I think about a word that I want to use and I look it up in the dictionary. Then I begin to *read* the dictionary!" Claire says she can amuse herself for hours this way,

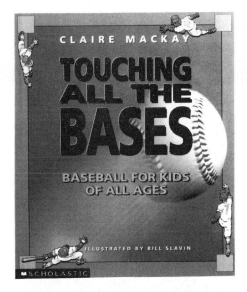

since she collects dictionaries and owns well over a hundred of them.

Claire Mackay has another important place in the Canadian writers' community. She is one of eleven founding members of the Canadian Society of Children's Authors, Illustrators and Performers (CANSCAIP), an organization devoted to encouraging people who are interested in becoming working professionals in these fields. "Since then, of course, it has grown immensely. It's now sixteen years old and has close to 350 professional members and close to 1,200 associate members. I've been astonished by its growth, but I think the growth validated the original impulse. Yes, we do need something for creators of young people's materials."

"If I can write a fine sentence in one day, I can be happy the whole day."

DO IT YOURSELF!

Claire Mackay believes strongly that writing poetry and verse is the best training for all writers. You must be aware of the rhythm, root and weight of the words you're using, and you must be able to use them effectively in a very structured way. She suggests that you try writing a sonnet, ballad, quatrain or rondo. Before you begin, ask your teacher to help you determine how each of these kinds of poems is constructed.

Kevin Major

SELECTED TITLES

Hold Fast
*(Canada Council Children's
Literature Prize, CLA Book of
the Year Award, Ruth
Schwartz Children's Book
Award)*
1978

Far from Shore
1980

Thirty-six Exposures
1984

Dear Bruce Springsteen
1987

Blood Red Ochre
1989

**Eating Between the
Lines**
*(CLA Book of the Year Award
for Children)*
1991

**Diana: My
Autobiography**
1993

*Vicky Metcalf Award winner,
1992*

Born:
September 12, 1949, in
Stephenville, Newfoundland

Home:
St. John's, Newfoundland

A hockey player and a Frank
Mahovlich fan, Kevin Major
still found time for reading when
he was young. And he didn't seriously begin to write until he was
teaching at a junior high school in
the 1970's. "There weren't many
books around that had characters in
them much like the characters that
were in my classroom — no really
contemporary Newfoundland novels, and very few Canadian ones."

Kevin says that it was this real-
ization, combined with his own
memories of the confusing and wor-
risome experiences of being a
teenager, which made him decide
to write for young people. Kevin
describes the acceptance of his
novel *Hold Fast* as a great relief —
after having tried without success
to have an earlier work published.

MOVING ON

What made Kevin finally decide
to discard that first effort and move
on? "It was a combination of things.
One, I kept getting all these rejections. A number of them did say: We
think you have potential as a writer,
but we don't think this particular
book is worth publishing. And I can
remember one letter saying: You
live in a very interesting place in
the world; can't you write about
real people and real situations? I
really hadn't done that with the first
effort, and I suppose all these things
were enough encouragement to
think that I could put it aside and
start fresh. I was really glad that I
did, and I'm very glad now that that
book wasn't published."

Although Kevin did take the
publisher's advice and begin writing about real people and real situa-

tions, he has never written about himself in his novels. "I have to say there's a little bit of me in each of them, I guess; a writer can't help but bring some of himself to the book. But I've never taken my own growing-up period and developed a story from that time, with myself disguised as the central character. There are some characters who in personality and temperament have a lot of me in them, but I've tended to take them out of my own particular time period and put them in a more recent era."

Eating Between the Lines

KEVIN MAJOR

Kevin prefers to work without any distractions, and even wears ear plugs if other people are in the house making noise. He tries to get in five solid hours of writing a day and rarely runs out of ideas.

However, he says, "If things are sort of stalled, what I will do is just take time away and read the whole

"If I go for periods of time and am unable to write, I get rather cranky."

DO IT YOURSELF!

In his book *Eating Between the Lines*, Kevin Major writes about a character who has a magic coin which enables him to go directly into the stories he's reading. Kevin suggests that you use that same coin to go into a favourite book and discover which characters you might become. Then write a story to describe what will happen.

---

thing through — what I've written so far — and try in some way to outline where this book is going in a total sense, so that I don't just get characters in situations and not know what's going to happen to them next."

When a manuscript is finished, Kevin sends it off to his editor and waits for his or her suggestions. "Sometimes it's quite difficult. I've had disagreements in the past with editors about things that, to me, were very important. And I've had to debate in my mind about how strongly I felt about these particular points and how much ground I could hold, bearing in mind that I know the editor comes with a fresh perspective on it. A very important part of publishing fiction is to work with the editor."

Kevin says that his first comic fantasy, *Eating Between the Lines*, was probably the most difficult time he's ever had working with an editor, because the first person who looked at it didn't like the manuscript at all. "That was, I suppose, the most crucial point in any editor/writer relationship. In that case, I came to the point of having to withdraw the book, change editors and move on, because I really had felt that I had done something good with this book and I wanted to see it published."

Once again displaying a terrific knack for knowing what to discard — or perhaps more important in this case — what *not* to discard, Kevin found another publisher who did like his novel and even won some awards when it was printed!

Michael Martchenko

 Illustrations only.

Born:
August 1, 1942, in Carcassone, France

Home:
Toronto, Ontario

Michael Martchenko describes his young self as a comic book addict. "I used to go around the neighbourhood trading; that was our thing. Not too many kids had TVs, I guess, so we used to carry a bag of 'traders' under each arm and off we'd go, trading comics."

Michael's favourites were always the ones with really great paintings on the covers, and he recalls being particularly fond of *The Lone Ranger* and *Tarzan*.

"I always knew what I wanted to do. I was always interested in art and drew. I used to fill notebooks drawing little sketches and I used to copy comic book characters. For every project in school, if I had the opportunity, I would illustrate."

It's no surprise to Michael, then, that he found his way into the business of enhancing stories with illustrations himself.

When Michael begins the illustrations for a story, this is what he does: "I read it once, and then I read it twice. Then I suddenly start getting mind pictures and I do what's called thumbnail sketches. I do them on twelve little squares that I've drawn — only about two inches high — and I just do it quickly; it's almost like if I don't do it fast enough, I'll lose it."

Michael then considers each thumbnail very carefully and makes any changes he feels are necessary. Then he does full-sized pencil sketches.

MORE BOOK FOR YOUR BUCK

Michael jokes about wanting to give his readers more book for their buck by including extra little things in his pictures. "I would say I'm inspired by what I read, but I also like to add a lot of things to the illustrations that are not necessarily covered in the story. Rather than just having a girl and a boy talking on the street, I might do some silly little scene going on behind them — nothing too distracting, but something that kids would get a kick out of."

When he was starting out, Michael's daughter, Holly, and her friend, Helen, used to give him valuable feedback. "I would do my pencil sketches and then I'd say, Okay guys, come here. Sit down and I'm going to read you a story and show you some drawings. And I would read a segment and put up the drawing. They would stare at it and I'd watch their reactions. Then I'd say, What do you think? or What's the matter with it?"

Michael found this input helpful — until Holly grew up. Now, he's more comfortable about what works and what doesn't work, so he relies only on the author and his publisher for suggestions.

Although Michael's sketches rarely require major changes, he understands about being flexible. For example, in the preliminary sketches for his first book, *The Paperbag Princess*, there was a picture of the princess punching Prince Ronald in the nose at the end of the story. But when Robert Munsch and the publisher opted for a less violent ending, Michael changed his sketches to show the princess skipping triumphantly off into the sunset.

Until very recently, Michael worked at an advertising agency during the day and did his books at night and on the weekends. Now a full-time illustrator, he's finding new ways of managing his time. "It took a while to get used to the fact that I could do this stuff during the day. And then I thought, I wonder if I *can* do this stuff during the day, maybe I'm strictly a nocturnal illustrator!"

Whichever hours he works, Michael is extremely dedicated to the quality of his work, and his readers appreciate that. In fact, one young fan actually sent Michael two dollars for doing such a good job! "I put all I can into it because there's nothing worse than having a book published, then looking at it and going: Oh, I wish I hadn't done that. Or: If only I'd done this and I didn't do it because I was rushing."

It's that kind of dedication and discipline which has kept Michael Martchenko happy and very, very busy.

Michael on his first book: "To me it was just another freelance job; I didn't know it was going to change my life."

DO IT YOURSELF!

When he was young, Michael Martchenko practiced drawing by creating new art for his favourite comics. He suggests you draw new pictures for the text of your favourite story.

Carol Matas

Born:
November 14, 1949, in
Winnipeg, Manitoba

Home:
Winnipeg, Manitoba

Carol Matas never really gave much thought to a career in writing. "I'd always wanted to be an actor; that was my goal in life. I went away to theatre school and I was acting in Toronto, where I happened to be hanging out with a group of actors who were writing. A number of them were writing plays, but some of them were also writing prose.

"They used to share their stories back and forth, very much like the kids do in schools today. We'd get together in the afternoon or for dinner and people would read what they'd written. One of these stories was a fantasy about a raindrop and I was so taken by it. I thought: that really sounds like fun, I think I'll try that. I went home and sat down and wrote my first story, which happened to be a fantasy. I never would have said: I'm going to write children's books. It just so happened that I wrote a fantasy and the protagonists were both children.

"I read it to my friends and they loved it; they thought it was great. So I thought: Well, okay, I'll write another one. I did that for years and the stories kept getting longer. The first one was about five pages; the next was maybe ten; the next one was fifteen."

Carol lost some of this momentum when she got married, and it wasn't until she was pregnant with her first child that she resumed her writing in earnest. The first novel she wrote was another fantasy, the second was *The Fusion Factor*.

"There was a point in there where I almost gave it up because I'd written two; I'd written the fantasy and I'd written *The Fusion Factor* [now retitled *It's Up to Us*] and I'd written a number of short stories and none of them were being published. I thought: Well, maybe it's time to give it up. But at that time somebody from Nelson offered me a contract for one of my short stories. They never did publish it, but I was so encouraged that I said: I won't give it up, and I kept plugging away at *The DNA Dimension*."

The DNA Dimension was accepted right away and *The Fusion Factor* soon found its way into print, too. And Carol decided that maybe she was destined to become a writer, and not an actor, after all.

COMBINING IDEAS

Where does Carol get her ideas? *The DNA Dimension* came about after Carol had watched the movie *Apocalypse Now*, and after she had seen a public television series dealing with the difficult choices we're forced to make as genetic engineering becomes more prevalent. She combined ideas from both to write a story about politicians who believe they're doing the right thing for the people, but aren't.

Today Carol takes her inspiration from whatever is interesting her at the moment. "I got interested in *Lisa* and *Jesper* because my husband started telling me stories about what had happened to his family during the war. Then I was given a book about the rescue of the Danish Jews. I didn't know anything about it, so I figured that most Canadian kids probably didn't know the story, either. I thought it was a really important story to tell."

Carol was right to think that young readers would want to know more about this important part of history. Since her stories about the Danish Jews were published, Carol has received all kinds of encouraging letters from kids,

describing how much they've enjoyed her books.

Carol recalls here her own connection with books when she was in school: "I'd eat my lunch, then I'd go up to my room and lie on my bed and read. That was my favourite thing to do at lunch hour. I guess it sort of calmed me down and got me ready for the afternoon. I really liked that quiet time. Even now when I'm touring schools, I wish I could do that. I wish at lunch hour somebody would let me go into a room by myself and lie down and read for half an hour!"

"Read a lot; that's what I did. It doesn't matter what you read — read everything; read what you like!"

DO IT YOURSELF!

Carol Matas prefers to write about things that interest her. What's interesting you the most right now? Write about that.

Lucy Maud Montgomery

SELECTED TITLES

Born:
November 30, 1874, in Clifton, Prince Edward Island

Died:
April 24, 1942

When she was nine years old, Lucy Maud Montgomery discovered that she could write poetry. She had been reading a book of blank verse at the time, and was inspired to write "Autumn," a piece which her father insisted "didn't sound much like poetry."

"This squelched me for a time," she wrote, "but if the love of writing is bred in your bones, you will be practically non-squelchable."

Some time later, Lucy Maud Montgomery did find the praise she so longed to hear. She had composed a song, which she then considered to be her masterpiece, and had the opportunity to recite part of it to a guest who happened to be a singer. After Lucy Maud Montgomery had finished her reading, she waited with bated breath for the singer's critique. She said,

"the words were very pretty." As Lucy Maud Montgomery recalled, "...to me it was the sweetest morsel of commendation that had ever fallen to my lot, or that ever has fallen since, for that matter. Nothing has ever surpassed that delicious moment."

When her mother died of consumption, Lucy Maud Montgomery went to live with her grandparents. She published her first stories during a year long stay with her father in Saskatchewan, when she was only sixteen years old. Like her Anne character, Lucy Maud Montgomery was thrilled by her success. "The moment we see our first darling brain-child arrayed in black type is never to be forgotten. It has in it some of the wonderful awe and delight that comes to a mother when she looks for the first time on the face of her first born."

DESCRIPTIONS OF HOME

With the exception of Peg Bowen in *The Story Girl*, none of Lucy Maud Montgomery's characters were based on real people. However, many of her settings were based on places near her home on Prince Edward Island. *Anne of Green Gables* began as an idea for a serial — a story which would be broken into segments and published in a woman's magazine over a number of issues. But the character of Anne appealed to Lucy Maud Montgomery in a way that none of her other characters had, and, having already decided what would happen in the story, she resolved to write her first book instead.

Anne of Green Gables was typed on a second-hand typewriter that Lucy Maud Montgomery said, "never made the capitals plain and wouldn't print 'w' at all." After five rejections from various publishers, she put the story away in an old hat box, planning one day to sell it in the originally intended serial format for thirty-five or forty dollars. Thankfully, though, when she did revisit the manuscript, Lucy Maud Montgomery decided to submit it one last time and found herself a publisher.

It was indeed hard work and perseverance that made Lucy Maud Montgomery the writer that she was. Her own recollections of the early days go something like this: "For five months I got up at six o'clock and dressed by lamplight. The fires would not yet be on, of course, and the house would be very cold. But I would put on a heavy coat, sit on my feet to keep them from freezing and with fingers so cramped that I could scarcely hold the pen, I would write my 'stunt' for the day. Sometimes it would be a poem in which I would carol blithely of blue skies and rippling brooks and flowery meads! Then I would thaw out my hands, eat breakfast and go to school.

"When people say to me, as they occasionally do, Oh, how I envy you your gift, how I wish I could write as you do, I am inclined to wonder, with some inward amusement, how much they would have envied me on those dark, cold, winter mornings of my apprenticeship."

Lucy Maud Montgomery died in 1942, but her books live on. They have been translated into seventeen languages, including Japanese, Hebrew and Icelandic, delighting readers around the globe. In fact, nearly half of the authors interviewed in this collection decided to become writers after reading books by Lucy Maud Montgomery, almost all of them citing *The Story Girl* as a personal favourite, a sentiment which was shared by Lucy Maud Montgomery herself.

> *When* **The New York Sun** *turned down one of her stories, Lucy Maud Montgomery said, "I flinched, as from a slap in the face, but went on writing. You see I had learned the first, last, and middle lesson — Never give up!"*

DO IT YOURSELF!

Lucy Maud Montgomery spent every opportunity honing her skill as a writer, writing more than 500 short stories in her lifetime. Get in the habit of spending even half an hour each day working on your own writing. You might even try writing a serial like the ones Lucy Maud Montgomery wrote, making up a few pages of a story every day, going on for as many weeks as you like.

Robin Muller

SELECTED TITLES

Mollie Whuppie and the Giant
1982

Tatterhood
1984

The Sorcerer's Apprentice
1985

The Lucky Old Woman
1987

Little Kay
1988

The Magic Paintbrush
(Governor General's Literary Award)
1989

The Nightwood
1991

 Hickory, Dickory, Dock
1992

Row, Row, Row Your Boat
1993

Little Wonder
1994

 Text only.

Born:
October 30, 1953, in Toronto, Ontario

Home:
Toronto, Ontario

Ask Robin Muller what he read when he was a boy and he'll tell you, "I read a combination of Shakespeare, *Winnie the Pooh*, *Rupert* annuals and *Freddy the Pig* which accounts for the twisted person that you meet today, and which probably explains why I can go from something as light and frivolous as *Row, Row, Row Your Boat* to something as dark and intense as *The Magic Paintbrush*."

Robin came to be a children's author and illustrator years after deciding to become an artist. "One reason I started getting into children's books — and now do children's books exclusively — was because I found being a visual artist and dealing with a single static image wasn't satisfying me. I wanted a narrative to the pictures, and

children's books were the best way to include the two."

When he's putting together a new book, Robin works from about nine o'clock in the morning until ten or eleven at night, but he doesn't believe these hours are too long. "As the day progresses you become more involved in the world on the piece of paper in front of you — it takes on a greater sense of being tangible than the real world." And although Robin does admit that actually getting started in the morning can be difficult, once he gets going, it's equally difficult to drag himself away at night.

TRYING TO REMEMBER

Kids often ask Robin where he gets his ideas, and he says, "I try to remember the things that moved me when I was their age. I try to remember the stories and situations that were a burden to me or helped me get through things, and these are the issues that I like to raise in my stories."

Unlike some illustrators, Robin does not like to get his ideas from the library. "I'm really sloppy with research because I like to be able to use my own visual vocabulary. I pride myself on being someone who actually observes quite well. I take in a lot and I'm always noticing things, but when I sit down to draw, I don't want to have my momentum disturbed by having to run to a book or run to the library or rely on photographs; I just like to be able to draw it. This is why sometimes my drawings are so incredibly inaccurate. When I have to try and figure out how a train works, I fake it. I could never illustrate a textbook for that reason, because I don't really like having to run out and use research material."

When his first book was published, Robin recalls that he wasn't completely happy with his illustrations, largely because creating children's books was so new to him. Now, though, he's less often disappointed with his work. "I can stand back and look at it and think: Robin, you did a good job there. I've covered up the problems better; I've smoothed it out."

In an ideal world, Robin would rather have a break before seeing his printed books. "I've always wished that when I finish a book, I wouldn't actually see it for about two years. That way I've completely forgotten it, so when I pick the book up and look at it, it's a fresh experience to me. Instead, from the point in time when I've finished it to when I get it back from the printer,

"You can have chapters of drivel in a novel, but in a picture book it has to be concise, clear and real poetry."

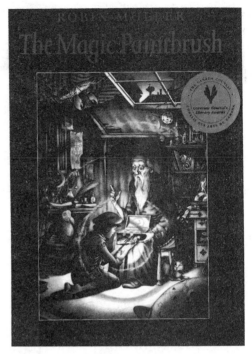

my imagination has actually improved all the illustrations. The colours are brighter and it's better drawn, so that when I see the actual thing — even though it looks exactly like the illustrations I submitted — I'm disappointed. I think, because I tend to work so obsessively, I really need the obsession to be over before I can come back and really like what I've done."

DO IT YOURSELF!

Robin Muller has had tremendous success using an old toothbrush as a paintbrush. He suggests you try to use something that you would never think to use to make a piece of art. You could, for example, colour with pastels or crayon, then scrape at the surface with an old plastic utensil.
Robin's one piece of advice: if you do decide to try his toothbrush idea, don't use your brother's toothbrush unless he's smaller than you are!

Robert Munsch

SELECTED TITLES

Mud Puddle
1979

The Paperbag Princess
1980

Thomas' Snowsuit
(Ruth Schwartz Children's Book Award)
1985

Love You Forever
1986

I Have to Go!
1987

A Promise Is a Promise
(co-author)
1988

Good Families Don't
1990

Something Good
1990

Purple, Green and Yellow
1992

Wait and See
1993

Vicky Metcalf Award winner, 1987

Born:
November 6, 1945,
in Pittsburgh, Pennsylvania, USA

Home:
Guelph, Ontario

When Robert Munsch was working in a childcare centre in 1974, he made up and told his young charges lots and lots of stories. And although he suspected that some of his stories were pretty good, he didn't submit them to a publisher until 1979, when he was working at the University of Guelph. The university's chairman had given him the summer off with orders to publish. "By the end of the summer, I had sent out ten stories to ten different publishers." But only one was interested. That publisher was Annick Press and the story was *Mud Puddle*.

"Most kids know that I put children from out there into my books. So almost all kids ask to be in them." In fact, Robert's next book began with a letter he received from a young reader. And in 1995 he'll be co-publishing a story with a girl who wrote him a letter when she was only eight (she's twelve now). At the time, his co-author had just moved to Scarborough from Beirut, and in her letter she described to Robert her first Halloween in Canada. Robert was so impressed with her letter that he began to correspond with her, and five letters later the two of them had written a story.

PRACTICE MAKES PERFECT

Robert's philosophy must be practice makes perfect, because he fine-tunes his stories (always with an audience) a hundred times or more before he's sure they're ready for his publisher. But Robert doesn't edit on paper. "The way I do a rewrite is I go out and get an audience. In fact, I don't even think of it as a rewrite. It's just that the story changes very slowly when I'm telling it and telling it and telling it."

When Robert is ready to try one of his stories on an audience, he refers to a list of schools which have sent him the most imaginative

by Robert Munsch   art by Michael Martchenko

letters, and picks one. He prefers to talk to one grade one or grade two class at a time when he's refining his material, because if the group is too large it loses its intimacy and becomes a show. After he's tried his main story on the group, Robert always offers to make up a story for one of the kids in the class.

"It's totally up for grabs, because I generally don't know what I'm going to say. I tend to make up a lot of stories about observable characteristics — hair colour, earrings, purple shoes — because I'm looking at a kid, thinking: What am I going to do now? "

Robert admits that these on-the-spot stories usually aren't that good, but once in a while — as his more than twenty-five books will attest — he comes up with something great. When he thinks he's hit on something, Robert will write to the kid who inspired his story and ask for a photograph, which he then keeps in a file with the story idea until he's ironed out all of the kinks.

It's very important to Robert to acknowledge the kids who inspire his stories. So, if and when he decides to go ahead with a story that's tied to a particular kid, he makes sure that his illustrator uses that child's photograph as reference for one of the characters in the book.

Another way Robert gets ideas is by staying with or visiting the people and places he plans to include in his books. He has, for instance, stayed with a family in a Hutterite colony after corresponding with a number of children who lived

The Paper Bag Princess

STORY · ROBERT N. MUNSCH
ART · MICHAEL MARTCHENKO

there. He's stayed with a wolf hunter in Chesterfield Inlet and will soon be staying with a lobster fisherman on Grand Manan Island.

Robert Munsch gets 10,000 fan letters a year from kids. The neatest letters he has ever received have been quilts and flags. The biggest letter he ever got was four metres tall and was a rolled-up picture of David's father from his book *David's Father*. And the longest letter he ever got was a scroll half a football field long. Needless to say, he was unable to open this one in the house!

"I'm like a stand-up comic, reacting to the audience."

DO IT YOURSELF!

If you want to write a story, tell it to three different friends first, then write it down. This will help you work out all of the bugs. It works for Robert Munsch!

Kit Pearson

SELECTED TITLES

The Daring Game
1986

A Handful of Time
(CLA Book of the Year Award
for Children)
1987

The Sky Is Falling
(CLA Book of the Year Award
for Children, Geoffrey Bilson
Award for Historical Fiction
for Young People)
1989

The Singing Basket
1990

Looking at the Moon
1991

The Lights Go on Again
1993

Born:
April 30, 1947, in Edmonton,
Alberta

Home:
Vancouver, British Columbia

K it Pearson's life was changed by a book. "When I was twelve, I read *Emily of New Moon* by L. M. Montgomery, which is about a child who wants to be a writer, and is based on Lucy Montgomery's life. After that, I decided I would be a writer, too; it had a profound influence on me."

However, after this revelation, Kit put off a career in writing until she was thirty-five. "I *wanted* to write all those years, but I was afraid to start, and I didn't know anybody who wrote. Then I became a children's librarian and I was just too busy. But I finally took a year off and went to Simmons College in Boston and got an M.A. in children's literature. Two of the courses I took were in writing for children and that really got me motivated. I left Simmons determined to start a book."

THE PERFECT AGE

It didn't take long for Kit to decide how old the characters in her novels would be. "I have a very strong memory of being nine to twelve especially. I loved being that age more than I liked being a teenager, so I write about that age." Kit's first book is about going away to boarding school and, although she drew on her own experiences at boarding school when she was a teen, her heroine is eleven and the story is told from a younger girl's point of view.

It can take between one and three years for Kit to write a novel, and during that time she may complete as many as five drafts. Kit doesn't begin with a conventional outline, though; instead, she prefers just to write and see what happens. She creates what she calls a kind of written outline, which includes much of the story, but leaves many gaps for description which will be filled in later. Kit also does a fair bit of planning before she begins, particularly when she's working on an historical novel. *The Sky Is Falling*, for instance, took nearly a year to research.

"My World War II books certainly started with people telling me about World War II. Alice Kane, who's a librarian in Toronto, told me how she used to tell stories to the kids who were evacuated to Canada, and that really got me thinking about these kids. I found out that some of my cousins almost sent their kids to stay with my grandparents, and that my mother knew war guests in

Toronto when she was living there during the war."

Kit's interest in the war guests — children who, for their own safety, were sent to stay with host families in other countries during the Second World War — snowballed until it seemed that she was finding information everywhere. She even took a trip to collect information that would help her create her characters. "I went to England and found a village for them to live in; I talked to people who were kids during the war; and I read newspapers of the time. The only thing I didn't do — and didn't want to do — was talk to people who were actually war guests, because the character of Norah was developing in my mind and I didn't want to write someone else's story.

"Once you get an idea planted in your mind, you're very alert to anything you hear about it."

decorations were like in 1940, not being able to do up the buttons on your fly if you were a little boy. I think it's the little tiny details that make a story much more real than the historical details."

Despite the long hours research requires, Kit never tires of it. "It was fun to research the World War II books. I think my problem with research is that because I'm a librarian I love research, and research is a great way of procrastinating. It was very hard to stop doing the research for *The Sky Is Falling*; I could have gone on forever. I kept thinking: I'll just read one more book and then I'll start."

But then Kit explains that she has always been a reader who couldn't resist just one more book. "When I was a child, I was such an avid reader that I actually ate the books! I used to tear off the bottom right hand corner or the top right hand corner and absent-mindedly put it in my mouth and chew it and swallow it. All my childhood books have the corners torn off." This certainly puts a new twist on the expression, "devouring a book"!

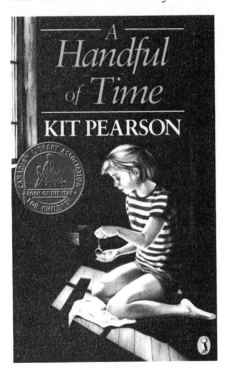

"I think the most helpful thing was talking to people who were kids during the war, because they supplied me with all kinds of tiny details that I wouldn't have been able to find: what the Christmas

DO IT YOURSELF!

Kit Pearson's first two novels and her trilogy end with her characters leaving one place and going to another. She suggests you write a letter or a series of letters from Eliza or Patricia or Norah or Gavin to someone they've left behind. What do you think happens to them in their new lives?

Gordon Penrose (Dr. Zed)

SELECTED TITLES

Dr. Zed's Brilliant Book of Science Experiments
1977

Dr. Zed's Dazzling Book of Science Activities
1982

Magic Mud and Other Great Experiments
1987

Dr. Zed's Science Surprises
1989

Dr. Zed's Sensational Science Activities
1990

More Science Surprises from Dr. Zed
1992

Born:
July 24, 1925, in Hamilton, Ontario

Home:
Scarborough, Ontario

How did Gordon Penrose become Dr. Zed? "When I started teaching, there were a lot of textbook experiments, but I became disillusioned with many of them because they didn't work. So, I started to create little experiments out of household materials (because elementary school teachers didn't have that much equipment) and I tried to make them so kids could go home and do them." Gordon Penrose certainly had a knack for devising interesting material. Not only were his students enthusiastic about his experiments, but so was one publisher.

WHEN IN ALL BEGAN

Gordon recalls, "On February 22, 1977, at two o'clock in the afternoon, Annabel Slaight knocked on my door at Beverley Acres School,

where I was working at the time, and asked me if I'd like to be Dr. Zed. That's how it all began. I was so overwhelmed, I said yes!"

As Dr. Zed, Gordon doesn't just write books of science experiments for kids. His ideas also appear in *Chickadee* and *Owl* magazines and on OWL/TV. How does one scientist come up with new and unusual ideas for so many audiences? "I have close to 500 books on science experiments, and I've collected well over 200 scientific toys. I study the books and I study the toys and I see what the principle is behind them. Then I see if I can develop something out of household materials using the same principle."

Remembering back to his teaching days, Gordon is also careful to think about his readers. "A lot of the books are very difficult for children to do, so when I look at something I say: What can I do to make this simple?"

One way of making sure that his experiments are simple is by testing them over and over again. In fact, Gordon often spends a very long time developing an idea before he's sure it will be fun and easy for every reader. "Sometimes everything happens like lightning and I just sit down and write it. Other times I keep working at it. There's an experiment — the warbling bird whistle I call it — I've been working on that thing for three and a half years now and it still isn't right. The thing is, you have to have it so it works every time for everyone, and that's the really difficult part. I get this thing working and I can do it, and then I have someone else do it and they run into problems. I'll just keep thinking of different ways of trying it. The result is so beautiful I want to keep working at it so that anyone can do it."

A second way Gordon keeps his experiments simple is by writing very detailed instructions.

"When I'm writing, I try to picture a person who doesn't know anything about it at all. (When I first became Dr. Zed I made too many assumptions about what people would know. It's funny, if you know something, you think everyone else does, too.)

"Then I take all the materials and the instructions and I have the people at *Owl* and *Chickadee* make the experiments. Then they adjust the instructions according to their experiences."

Gordon also gets a lot of suggestions from his young fans. (He recently made his 3,100th school visit.) He's so appreciative of their help that he donates half the proceeds of his work to children's charities around the world.

Suggestions aside, Gordon does sometimes hit a brick wall. "As I'm going along, if I'm getting frustrated I put the experiment up on the shelf so I can see it to think about it, but I don't pursue it because I don't want to end up with the experiment working, but me feeling rotten about it. I think about it when I'm in bank line-ups or waiting for stop lights, and I come back and try it again. I keep doing that until I get it."

If Gordon could pick the one thing that makes him glad to be Dr. Zed, it would be the feeling he gets when an experiment works. "I can feel this radiating joy when an experiment works. It's just… WHOOPEE!!"

"What I really love is surprises. I used to do all these things to create surprises for myself when I was young."

DO IT YOURSELF!

Gordon Penrose suggests you make an experiment your own by going over the instructions for an existing experiment and changing one or two things. It's best if you only change one thing at a time so you can be sure of what works. Then write down how to do your experiment in your own words, give your instructions and the necessary materials to a friend, and let that friend test away.

Stéphane Poulin

Born:
December 6, 1961, in Montreal, Quebec

Home:
Montreal, Quebec

Stéphane Poulin was first approached to do work as a children's book illustrator and author at an art exhibition in Montreal. Although he still maintains that he cannot write — "I'm not really a writer, and I hate it " — he accepted Tundra's unusual challenge to both write and illustrate a book for kids.

"It was great. My first book was the ABC book *Ah! Belle Cité/A Beautiful City ABC*. They asked me to do the text and the illustrations and the whole conception of the book, which was a very special treat because there was nobody to tell me what to do and how to do it. I was totally free to do what I wanted to do."

After enjoying the opportunity to handle so many different aspects of the production, Stéphane contin-

ues to write his own stories today, because he would rather not wait for stories to come to him, and because as both author and illustrator he has the freedom to draw whatever he likes.

The biggest problem for Stéphane the writer is fleshing out the middle of a story. "All my stories are built like jokes. You have a beginning and a big end, but the middle is not really important. It's tough for me to develop the story and make it longer."

But if Stéphane has trouble with the middle of a book when he's writing, that's where he reaches his stride when he turns into Stéphane the illustrator. Stéphane says that he learns new tricks after he's finished the first few illustrations of a book, and admits that as he nears the end he often becomes exhausted. So, in order to prevent his books from looking great in the middle and rough on both ends, Stéphane never does his paintings in order.

ONE AT A TIME

He's also careful to do his paintings one at a time to avoid feeling as though he were working on an assembly line. And Stéphane has another reason for this approach, too. "In a way, if I work on more than one piece at a time I will repeat the same atmosphere. I prefer to do a complete atmosphere for one and then when it's over I pass to the second one."

Stéphane began using oil paints when he was working on his first book. At that time, he and his wife had just had their first son, Gabriel, and were sharing the work of caring for the baby. Oil paints dry slowly, allowing Stéphane to leave his work to change diapers and soothe tears without risking disaster. He's used oils ever since.

When kids ask him which of his books is his favourite, Stéphane tells them, "*Benjamin and the Pillow Saga* is actually the book I prefer because of the spirit of the book. It's very quiet. It's very dark, too. I made that book at a moment where I was happy about my technique. Technically, I was happy."

Stéphane no longer does school visits, however, saying, "It's very difficult because people expect a lot from you when you go to visit and I'm not an entertainer. I hate to entertain; I feel like I am selling toothpaste. I wish I could be with kids for three or four hours and

STEPHANE POULIN

"I think if people could work in a place where they could explore their real interests we would have a beautiful world."

draw, but I always feel the pressure to read and make kids laugh, which is very artificial."

Stéphane's earlier Josephine books took only about a month to do, but now, as he tries for cleaner, more detailed pictures, Stéphane finds that he needs around eight months to complete a project. Stéphane works only four days a week, saying he doesn't learn much by working all the time. He devotes the rest of his time to his family, explaining, "Being with my children is very very important."

DO IT YOURSELF!

Stéphane Poulin has discovered that pushing yourself to try something new sometimes helps you to develop an existing skill. If you consider yourself to be an artist, try to develop your skill as a writer. You may find that it helps you think more clearly about what to include in your illustrations.

Barbara Reid

SELECTED TITLES

 Illustrations only.

Born:
November 16, 1957, in
Toronto, Ontario

Home:
Toronto, Ontario

Barbara Reid has been playing with Plasticine ever since she was in elementary school, where she used it to create models for practically every project she was assigned. A particularly memorable piece for Barbara was a model she made of an entire maple sugar bush!

For Barbara, the decision to earn her living as an artist was made in an instant. Barbara had never planned to become a professional illustrator: at her high school, art was considered to be something of a joke. But she abruptly changed her mind when, on career day, a couple of students from the Ontario College of Art came to speak at her school. Barbara admits that at first she was drawn into the presentation merely because the presenters happened to be "really cute guys,"

but it was the thought that she could do what she loved for a living that sold her on the idea. And so, in grade thirteen, risking ridicule from her peers, Barbara Reid enrolled at the Ontario College of Art.

There, Barbara's favourite area of study was art history. In fact, she's still interested in the puzzle of who an artist really is — looking in every piece for clues about the artist and about what he or she is trying to say. In her own work, Barbara says that she is usually making fun of something that is serious or pompous; she thinks of herself as a cartoonist.

EARLY DISAPPOINTMENTS

Barbara's first publishing experiences weren't as exciting as her current efforts. She did a lot of textbooks and other small jobs to help her pay the bills. Sometimes these projects were discouraging because the paper and printing weren't the best (authors and illustrators who are just starting out often work on small, cheaply produced books until they gain some experience), and she felt that her artwork never looked as good on the printed page as it did in her original. In particular, she found the colours dull or inaccurate, and it was often disappointing to see these unchangeable mistakes. Barbara has, with time, learned not to take these disappointments to heart. She tries to look at her finished books as a consumer would, and that — coupled with the better paper and printing techniques that are available to her today —

makes her feel a lot happier about her publishing experiences.

Kids often ask Barbara: How do you get the Plasticine into the book? She explains that the Plasticine isn't actually *in* the book. Instead, Barbara's Plasticine art is photographed and it's those photos that appear on the printed page. The photographs are vital to the way the book will look, so Barbara and her photographer husband spend a great deal of time setting up the lights and framing the shots.

The other question young artists ask Barbara is, Where do you get all

of those colours of Plasticine? Barbara doesn't buy all of the colours you see in her books, she mixes them. She admits that some of the colours available are really dull, so she "cheats" to make them seem brighter. She puts yellows beside blues, employing all of the tricks of contrasting colours, which, she explains, is another technique she learned at art college.

Recently, Barbara had the opportunity to illustrate *and* write a picture book, and she says she learned a lot in the process. "Writing is hard work," explains Barbara. "Illustrating is *enjoyable* hard work." Barbara confesses that her experience taught her that she prefers to work on the illustrations only, spending her time reshaping an idea or solving the problem of illustrating someone else's tale. For jobs like those, Barbara exclaims, "Writers are my heroes! I'm just decorating the story."

Barbara's illustrations are big and heavy. They can weigh anywhere between two and an incredible seven kilograms and must be stored individually, so Barbara packs each into its own pizza box for safekeeping. Needless to say, Barbara doesn't have enough room at home to take all of the "pages" of her books out and look at them together, so she really enjoys having an art show once in a while. And because she doesn't have enough room at home to keep every single piece, Barbara sells her art after her books are printed, saying "I'm more attached to the books than I am to the art."

"If you want to draw something, you have to look at it."

DO IT YOURSELF!

Here's an idea from Barbara Reid, art history buff: Do a portrait of someone and include in the portrait something that tells about that person's activities or interests.
For example, if the person has a pet rabbit, he or she could be holding a carrot in the portrait.

Barbara Smucker

SELECTED TITLES

Henry's Red Sea
1955

Susan
1970

Underground to Canada
1977

Days of Terror
(Canada Council Children's Literature Prize, Ruth Schwartz Children's Book Award)
1979

Amish Adventure
1982

White Mist
1985

Jacob's Little Giant
1987

Incredible Jumbo
(IODE Violet Downey Book Award)
1990

Garth and the Mermaid
1992

Vicky Metcalf Award winner, 1988

Born:
September 1, 1915, in Newton, Kansas, USA

Home:
Bluffton, Ohio, USA

Barbara Smucker recalls one of her first writing experiences: "My best friend and I wrote a novel together in longhand. It was a romance about a prince and a princess. We were too shy to let anyone else read it. I remember going out to the field with a shovel, digging a hole for the book, then putting a rock on it to remember the place." The book was not there when she returned fifty years later to dig it up. An apartment building was in its place.

Barbara studied to become a journalist and later worked for a local newspaper, but her next significant publishing experience didn't come for many years. "I heard the story from a man who was visiting our home. Our children were very small at that time and they listened so intently to this story that I thought it really should be written for children and not be just an incident that was recorded in the newspaper. So, I wrote it with a seven- or eight-year-old boy in mind — Henry I called him." The book was *Henry's Red Sea*.

Barbara then approached her Mennonite church's publisher. "It was one of the first children's books that they published. And I was pretty excited about it. I'd written newspaper stories and short stories, but I'd never had a book published. I remember getting it in the mail one day when it was finished and I was so excited and nervous I could hardly hold it. It's a very thrilling event in a writer's life to publish a first book."

AN EDITOR'S SUGGESTIONS

The publishing experience has always been an enjoyable one for Barbara. "I've been very fortunate to have two excellent editors; they've been very knowledgeable about the book field and have been very very helpful. I tell them what I'm working on, then I try to complete the whole manuscript. When I'm writing, I realize it isn't the way it's going to be when it's finished. My editors have made outstanding suggestions — sometimes I've used them and sometimes I haven't. They haven't made me feel that I'm compelled to change my manuscripts the way they want them to be."

"Most of the books I write for young people are called historical fiction. They are stories about true, important and dramatic events in history and I have them happen to imaginary boys and girls and their families."

Barbara has always found it helpful to read her stories aloud. "Once I was in a writers' group, where we read things aloud to each other. You could only be in this writers' group if you had published, so they were serious writers. And that was helpful, too, because no one hesitated about being highly critical. Sometimes it was difficult to be there — sometimes you almost hated to read your material — but it was really helpful. I do think the input of another person is important for a writer. At least it has been for me."

Barbara visits schools all over Canada and is amazed at the number of kids she meets who are new to this country. She marvels at the great work they and their teachers are doing with books, and she encourages them all to look back into their own family histories for story ideas.

DO IT YOURSELF!

Barbara Smucker's books are based on true stories that she has heard. She suggests you interview your grandmother or grandfather or some older person you know and do a little story research. Ask what their lives were like when they were your age. What did they wear? What did they study? What sports or games did they play? What important world events were happening then?

Ted Staunton

SELECTED TITLES

Born:
March 29, 1956, in Toronto, Ontario

Home:
Port Hope, Ontario

For Ted Staunton, making up stories is a habit that goes back to his childhood. "I would read long before my parents were awake. And at night, I remember, for a long time I would make up stories to tell to myself after the light was turned out. This was incredibly frustrating at times, because what would happen was I'd get part way, and then I'd fall asleep. So I'd never continue the story and I'd have to start over again the next night. It was like editing."

Despite this penchant for making up stories as a kid, Ted hated writing when he was in school. He did, however, love to read, and he loved those days when the teacher would read to the class. He believes that it's this love of reading which eventually turned him into a writer.

"If you want to be a writer you have to be a reader first, because when it comes time for you to write you'll know that you're ready. Part of the reason you'll know is that you won't feel quite so intimidated, because you've read thousands of beginnings and thousands of endings and thousands of other ways to say: She said."

AN IDEAL WORK DAY

Ted describes his idea of an ideal work day: "If I'm planning a book, there's no schedule at all. Because I never can tell where I'm going to make the connections or get the ideas, I might as well be cutting the lawn. If I'm writing, I aim for being at my desk for about the length of the school day — from about nine to about three-thirty.

"But I really have to be into the flow of a book for it to happen. Most of my time is spent looking forward to the day when I'll be able to sit down for those six or seven hours. Meanwhile, I've still got to come up with an ending or understand a character, so I might as well cut the lawn again." In fact, if you're curious to know just how obsessed with lawn maintenance Ted can become when he's experiencing writers' block, take a look at Cyril's dad in *Mushmouth and the Marvel*, because that character is actually based on Ted.

There's a fair bit of Ted to be found in the pages of many of his books. "The character of Cyril is based on me when I was in grade school. I was a very shy and retiring type like Cyril. But more than the things that happen to Cyril, it's Cyril's outlooks or his desires that echo mine. So that if Cyril really, really wants a good part in the school play and he's constantly overlooked, that's because that's the way I felt. Or if he really wants somebody's attention or approval, it's because that's the way I felt. But how he goes about that or what happens to him is practically always based on either someone else's life or on something I've made up."

Or it may be based on something that Ted has read. The research challenge for the Maggie and Cyril books was that he needed to figure out problems and solutions a character of Maggie's age and background would be able to handle. "Often in the early days, what I would do to generate some ideas for those books would be to go to the library and get the kinds of books that I thought Maggie would read. I

assumed that she was a reader of nonfiction, for sure: she'd be into facts books, science books, statistics books, how-to books, and I would record in my notebook ideas that might come in handy."

From there Ted gets down to business and begins those six or seven hours of writing. "The smallest room in our house is my office, and I've got a desk, I've got my computer and I've got my reference books. I wrote all the novels and picture books, except for the newest one, on a manual portable typewriter. But I finally gave in and bought a computer — and it's great. What a fool I was! My publishers love it because before I couldn't be bothered retyping everything, so I would just type out the new paragraph and staple it on top. They'd get stuff that looked like…well, it was just awful. *But* they *looked* like real manuscripts!"

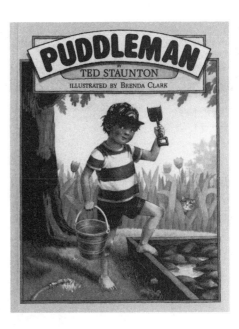

"The chaos of my mind is compensated for by an obsession with having an orderly house."

DO IT YOURSELF!

Ted Staunton suggests you plan a story by working up a storyboard. Most picture books have the same number of pages for reasons that make their manufacture easier and more economical. So, picture book authors know in advance how many pages of writing their books are going to have to be. Get a piece of paper and draw lines to divide it into eight sections (each will represent one page of your book) and then begin to draft your story by jotting notes in each of the boxes. You may already know, for instance, how you want it to end and maybe one or two things that will happen in the middle. Fill those in first and then use these as clues to help you map out the rest of the book.

Cora Taylor

SELECTED TITLES

Julie
(Canada Council Children's Literature Prize, CLA Book of the Year Award for Children)
1985

The Doll
(Ruth Schwartz Children's Book Award)
1987

Julie's Secret
1991

Ghost Voyages
1992

The Summer of the Mad Monk
1994

Born:
January 14, 1936, in Fort Qu'Appelle, Saskatchewan

Home:
Winterburn, Alberta

Cora Taylor grew up as the only child in a family of avid readers, but as much as she remembers being encouraged to indulge in the habit, she also recalls being told to put the books aside. "I do remember being kicked out all the time when I was a kid because you weren't supposed sit around reading; it was not a productive activity. So in the wintertime they would say: You can't be sitting around with your nose in a book all the time. Go outside and get some roses in your cheeks.

"Roses in your cheeks were very big. I, unfortunately, didn't have a roses-in-your-cheeks complexion, and no matter what I did — short of frostbite — they really weren't rosy. So I would smuggle my book out underneath my ski jacket and go and huddle up in the caboose.

"Now you probably don't know what a caboose is. You think it's on the end of a train, don't you? Well, not in the Prairies. In the wintertime in those days you couldn't drive your car because the roads were not good, so everybody put their cars up on blocks, drained their radiators and said goodbye to their cars until spring. Instead you drove a caboose, which was a horse-drawn, covered sled with a stove in it."

Cora says she didn't actually use the stove, for fear of giving herself away, but she did spend those cold hours outdoors tucked under blankets reading as much as she pleased. "I'd sit outside and read until I was nearly frozen!"

Cora had many aspirations when she was a girl. "I had a lot of unrealistic ambitions when I was a child, and they changed and became more and more realistic along the way. Aside from being a fairy princess and then a movie star, being an author came third. By that time I had learned not to tell anybody."

Abandoning her dream to become a movie star when she was told that her nose was too big, Cora resolved that her ambition to become an author would remain a secret to prevent people from telling her what she then believed to be true — that it was an impractical occupation.

PURSUING A SECRET AMBITION

It has turned out to be anything but impractical for Cora, though. In fact, she is perfectly suited to her chosen career. Always fascinated with family history, she's been able time and again to go back to her memories and draw on ideas for her stories. For instance, there really is a doll named Jessie that Cora was allowed to hold only when she was sick. That, of course, was the model for *The Doll*.

Another particularly fond family recollection is that of her mother's older sister, Beth, who was much loved by everyone and who died young before Cora was even born. To Cora, Beth was always a romantic figure. She was buried in her wedding dress and her tombstone was carved from a stone near the place where she and her husband used to walk. But the topper for Cora was that Beth died of consumption. "Keats had consumption. The Bröntes had consumption. Beth had a literary disease!"

And when snooping in the secret compartment of a desk revealed old letters written by Beth, who suddenly became a real, fun person, Cora made the final connection that caused her to become an author: "If you write, if you leave something behind, people who otherwise would never get to know you *would* get to know you." Years later, memories of trips with her grandmother to Beth's grave would inspire other scenes in Cora's book *The Doll*.

Cora began work on her first novel when she was in school as an adult student. She had intended to write it as a book for adult readers. But as rewrite followed rewrite — every one beginning with a fresh start — Cora decided that the story was better described as a novel for children, and eventually found a publisher who was interested.

"The rewriting was a lot of work. I think the most annoying part was that I got my first computer at that point and I would finally write something that I really liked and then it would die and go away, and I'd have to sit down and rewrite that. And there's still a scene in there that's not as good as one that's in computer heaven!"

"As a kid I was a terrific snooper. I was a neat snooper. Kids nowadays just do not know how to snoop. You go in a room and you know they've been in there. I could snoop and nobody would know."

DO IT YOURSELF!

Cora Taylor suggests this story-writing tactic: Think of three unrelated things, then challenge yourself to somehow tie all three together in one story.

Gilles Tibo

SELECTED TITLES

Simon and the Snowflakes
1988

Simon and the Wind
1989

Simon Welcomes Spring
1990

The King of Sleep
1991

Simon in Summer
1991

Mr. Clark's Summer Holiday
1992

Paper Nights
1992

Simon and his Boxes
(Governor General's Literary Award)
1992

Mr. Patapoum's First Trip (co-author)
1993

 Castle Chaos
1993

 Illustrations only.

Born:
July 18, 1951, in Nicolet, Quebec

Home:
Montreal, Quebec

G illes Tibo talks about his early experiences as an artist. "When I was very young, I was already interested in drawing and painting. By the time I was ten, I knew I wanted to be an illustrator. I was very disciplined, making two or three drawings in a big book every day, adding the date and sometimes a brief text.

"I was also turned on to the magic of print very early. I adored the smell of ink given off by the newspapers we got at home, and I thought it was fantastic that the illustrations and the comic strips I looked at were reproduced by the tens of thousands and distributed all over, in the cities and the countryside."

His fascination with comics continued until, at the age of sixteen, Gilles published some of his humorous drawings in a local paper. At the age of eighteen he published his first book — a 40-page comic strip. "I was involved in every stage of its production, which was my introduction to graphics and printing. It was by rubbing shoulders with people in the trade, by reading, asking questions, and above all by looking at everything that was published around me, that I learned my trade. I produced more than 2,000 humorous drawings and about 700 daily comic strips, contributing to most of the magazines and all the newspapers in Quebec."

How was it then, that a successful cartoonist moved into the business of publishing books for children? "In 1975, during a promotional tour, I happened to meet a children's book publisher with whom I produced my first six books for young people. That was a real revelation: I was able to give free rein to my two passions, illustration and graphics. I also worked with several authors who introduced me to their styles and to their fictional worlds."

Gilles had discovered a new fascination and in 1984 wrote and illustrated his first book for children. "I still illustrate my own stories, alternating that with projects submitted by publishers."

For those books that he does write on his own, Gilles finds inspiration in a number of different ways. "The approach and the story for every one is very different. Sometimes it starts with a vague, general idea about the subject, then

I add a beginning and an end, and stir until it has the desired consistency. Or else the character may be so vivid I'll simply let it come to life on the page. Other times, I'll create the entire story and then gradually, as I'm reworking it by myself or with the publisher, I'll arrive at a final version that's completely different from the first one."

Simon in summer

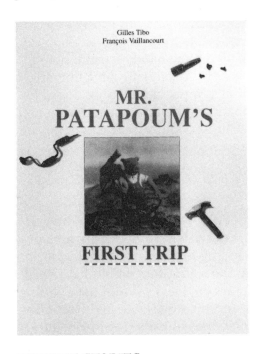

Gilles Tibo
François Vaillancourt

MR. PATAPOUM'S

FIRST TRIP

BEDTIME STORIES

Some of Gilles's books began as bedtime stories he told his son. "I'd make up a different story every night, and it was like a workshop in

"I have only one piece of advice for young people who would like to become authors and illustrators: Work, work and work some more! There is, unfortunately, no other way."

improvisation. Sometimes I'd be going along when a character would burst into the middle of a story and come back a few days later. Then the secondary characters and their adventures would join the original cast."

Wherever else he may get his ideas, Gilles Tibo does not draw on real life. "My fictional world is totally invented. I like characters that are a little wild and don't behave like other people. That allows me to create an imaginary world, to play tricks with logic, to present a world where anything is possible, something like the world inhabited by children when they play."

DO IT YOURSELF!

Gilles Tibo does not like to work in an opaque medium, instead preferring an air brush to help him achieve a light, almost transparent effect. Even if you don't have your own air brush, you can experiment with a similar effect. Arrange a number of small flat objects on a sheet of paper (buttons or coins, for example). Then dip a toothbrush in some paint and with your thumb strum the bristles to spritz paint all over the paper. Finally, remove the objects to reveal your work.

Ian Wallace

SELECTED TITLES

 Illustrations only.

Born:
March 31, 1950, in Niagara Falls, Ontario

Home:
Toronto, Ontario

From the age of four, Ian Wallace was well on his way to becoming an artist. "I always loved to draw and it wasn't always in the places I should have been drawing, like paper. It was on bedroom walls and even in the covers of books."

When he was thirteen, Ian decided to become an artist in earnest, even though, at the time, he didn't quite know what the life of an artist entailed. He carried that desire right through to college, where he began to search for his own particular place in the art community.

"I felt the education I was getting at college when I was in graphic design was too narrow, and so focused on design it didn't take in the whole creative process. So I began to move out and embrace all the disciplines possible within that college, and upon graduation I was a master of many things, but a master of nothing. BUT, I had learned to think and that, to me, is the bottom line of all creativity. That sounds rather clichéd, but I learned that all creative activity begins in the head first and the hands second. Before I went to art school I thought it all began in the hand. I didn't imagine that I would have to use my brain or think about what I was doing and why I was doing it."

THE RIGHT PLACE AT THE RIGHT TIME

After graduation, Ian had what he describes as the happy luck of finding himself in the right place at the right time, which happened to be the local student bar. "Sitting to my right was one of the founding members of Kids Can Press. She was talking that evening about the press and what it was trying to do, and how there were no books in this country for kids, published by Canadian writers and illustrators. I became intrigued and interested in the idea of working there for the summer. I thought it would be an interesting way to pass two months, but realized within three weeks of being hired on that project, not only did I wanted to draw, but I wanted to write, too."

Over time, Ian has learned that although picture books are relatively short, each requires a great deal of work. "In terms of quality, I think that you really can only produce one, hopefully fine, book each year.

I would be really hard pressed to go through all the things I need to do to in a shorter span of time."

One of the time-consuming things Ian feels he must do when he writes is, as he describes it, "get under the skin of those characters," fine-tuning his work until every one is just right. For instance, his revisions for *Chin Chiang and the Dragon's Dance* were so extensive that the stack of manuscript pages stood about 30 cm high and the paper weighed about seven kilograms. Yet there are only 160 lines of text in the finished book!

Ian says, "You have to have the courage and the patience and the tenacity to know when to go back to that story, to know when to put it away, to know when to take it out, to know when to drop portions and passages and themes and elements that are not working, when to draw back, and when to come in like gang busters."

One of Ian's biggest worries as an artist is correctness. "In books like *Chin Chiang and the Dragon's*

Dance and *Very Last First Time*, I was dealing with completely different cultures, different landscapes, different histories and different societies. The kind of responsibility that was on me was enormous because as Newfoundlanders would say, I'm 'from away.' Even when I was doing my latest book, T*he Mummer's Song*, I felt somewhat nervous about being 'from away,' and that's a good emotion to feel because it keeps you on your toes and you make sure with every ounce of your energy that the story is told with the dignity and respect due that culture."

Ian was recently asked if he might consider doing a version of *Hansel and Gretel*. His initial reaction was "no" because, as far as he could see, there already were classic versions in existence. Why reinvent the wheel? Ian changed his mind, though, when his editor convinced him that for each generation there is a new version that readers embrace. His editor also imparted a few wise words that apply to more than this project, telling Ian "you have something to say with everything that you do."

"I need the quiet solitude of time to write and illustrate, but I also have to be that gregarious performer who goes out and shakes and rattles and rolls kids and hangs them from the ceiling."

DO IT YOURSELF!

Ian suggests you experiment with different media (paints, pencils, markers, crayons, etc.). Do an illustration, then draw the same picture again, this time using a different medium. How does changing the medium change the look of the picture?

Eric Wilson

Born:
November 24, 1940, in Ottawa, Ontario

Home:
Victoria, British Columbia

Eric Wilson began his writing career when he was a teacher. "I was working with grade eight students in B.C. — kids who didn't like to read at all, and didn't seem to know much about Canada. That's what gave me my two principal goals, which were to write about Canada and to write books that would get kids into reading."

Over the years, Eric has discovered exactly the best way to develop books that accomplish just those goals. "I select a location and go and live there, then try and incorporate into my stories as many of my own personal experiences as possible."

WRITER ON LOCATION

For example, in his preparations for his new book, which will be a story about Tom Austen on an exchange trip from Winnipeg to Gjoa Haven, Eric joined a group of junior high school students on a winter exchange in that very same arctic town. They went out with dog sled teams and built igloos and Eric made a particular effort to get to know the people and their community. "Like the students, I was billeted with a family and so we got to eat caribou and that sort of thing. All those experiences will go into my story."

Eric also carries a tape recorder on these excursions to dictate notes and to record as much of the moment as he can. "For example, when we were out with the dog sled teams on the ice, I had the microcassette with me. I was muttering into it as we bumped and banged across the ice so that I could

get the actual sounds of the dogs and the sled runners in the snow." He wanted to capture every detail of that thrilling ride and try to reproduce it in his story.

"That, essentially, is what the research is; it's going to a real place and writing about it. That's why when I talk to kids in schools I always say, If you're going to do a story, begin by writing about some place that you know, namely your own neighbourhood or your own town."

When his field work is complete, Eric takes all that raw data home, where he spends between two and four months assembling it, thinking about his characters, and sorting related information into separate files on his computer. "For example, I'll have a scene that takes place at the school in Gjoa Haven, and so all the research that I did at the school I'll assemble in one file in my computer. Then when I come to do the actual writing, I'll go through that material and pick out what I think is the most interesting and telling information."

When it finally comes time to write the first draft of his new story, Eric will do the same thing he always does when he's writing; he'll cut himself off from every distraction. "When I'm going to be writing, I switch off the phone, hang a Do Not Disturb sign on the door of my apartment, and close all of the curtains so that I cut off my beautiful view of the Pacific Ocean and the mountains. The only light on in my apartment is a little tiny light glowing over my computer keyboard, so it's like a dark little cave. I like to be in that cave, so that when I'm writing my story I'm

ERIC WILSON
A Tom Austen Mystery
The Prairie Dog Conspiracy

in Gjoa Haven rather than in Victoria."

It takes Eric about two months to complete his first draft, which he then prints out ten times for what he describes as ten really important editors — five girls and five boys in grades four through eight from a school in Victoria. "They take the story home with them and they keep a diary. At the end of each chapter, they stop and write down the answers to several questions for me, including who they think the villain is and why, because this is a test-read for the clues." Eric also asks them to let him know where he's used dated language and where they think the story gets boring. "In other words, those ten kids read the story on behalf of all the kids who will read it as a book."

Then, of course, Eric works with his editor from HarperCollins, and after another couple of months of work, his manuscript is finally ready for his publisher. Not a bad system, really. Since Eric's books have been wildly popular with thousands of kids across Canada and as far away as Spain and Japan, one can't help but agree that he is indeed achieving his goals!

"I don't have children, but I like to think of my readers as my kids."

DO IT YOURSELF!

Accurate description is very important to Eric Wilson, so he's always very careful to describe not only what is seen but also what can be heard, smelled, touched and tasted. Try to remember to include descriptions of all of the things your characters sense the next time you write a story.

Janet Wilson

SELECTED TITLES

 Daniel's Dog
1990

 Jess Was the Brave One
1991

 Revenge of the Small Small
1992

 Gopher Takes Heart
1993

 How to Be Cool in the Third Grade
1993

 Howard's House Is Haunted
1993

The Worm Song and Other Tasty Tunes
1993

 The Baritone Cat
1994

 Tiger Flowers
1994

Text only.

 Illustrations only.

Born:
November 20, 1952, in Toronto, Ontario

Home:
Toronto, Ontario

Although she worked on her school's yearbook design and was co-creator of a special mural which is still on display in her old junior high, Janet Wilson never had the confidence to take her work as an artist seriously.

"Looking back on it, the ability was always there. I would do things and they'd look pretty good, but I always thought: Well, that was just a fluke, whereas somebody else would say: *It's* good because *I'm* good."

Janet believes that without encouragement and confidence, the only way to succeed is to change your attitude. And that's exactly what she did when, at the age of twenty-nine, she went to college for the first time to become an artist.

Encouraged by friends who were already working as professional illustrators, Janet was determined to make as much of this learning experience as she could. "I had maturity enough to know that when I graduated I had to be as good as the people who were out there already. So I made a real effort to learn and improve on each assignment. I had a drive because I knew what professional standards were."

Success came when Janet was approached by the art director at Scholastic to do her first picture book. "I had no idea when I started it what I was getting myself into." Janet had already had an easy time doing educational books, requiring twelve pictures each, and she thought that the thirty-two illustrations required for a picture book would be just as easy to do.

STARTING OVER

But Janet soon realized that story books are far more complicated than that; there has to be a common style throughout. "I got into the book — I think I had done about five pages — and I didn't like it. I thought, I can't carry this through the whole book! Each picture was so different. I had to change to a style that would be suitable for every page; so, I started over. I went through about four pages and I started to panic again. I thought, No, this isn't working either. I ended up starting that book over three times!"

Today, Janet doesn't let a problem go that far, but instead makes a clean start by breaking her board over her knee to prevent her from fiddling with it. "I start more pictures over than you can even imagine. I can spend two weeks on a painting that has to be handed in in two days, and if I don't like it, I'll start over. It's sickening, but it always looks better. Always!"

So how does Janet know when she's on track? "It's hard to describe, but every book tells you what to do; it speaks to you so that — in my books anyway — you'll notice that they aren't all the same style. I really feel that the book dictates how it's going to look. I wasn't listening to that in the beginning, but now I listen to it. I know more and more, *as* I do them, *how* to do them."

A particular favourite of Janet's, and a perfect example of a book dictating its own style, is her new

"If it's not working right from the beginning, you're only repairing it. You need to make a good start."

DO IT YOURSELF!

Here's an art activity from Janet Wilson. On a piece of paper make three unconnected squiggles. Then, pass your paper to someone else and challenge that person to join the lines to create a picture.

quilt story. She painted all of the pictures on canvas so the borders could be quilted, and she did a lot of research. "It takes place in the Mennonite community in Kitchener. So I went there and I spoke to Mennonites. I went to a quilting bee; I went to a museum; and I sort of immersed myself into the culture. There are so many things you have to think about. Like, for instance, What would a little girl wear to bed? Would she have a nightgown? Would she wear a hat? Would she tie the ribbons in her hair in bows? Or would they be strings? All these things you don't necessarily need to write about, but if it's in a picture and it's not accurate, people are going to notice."

Janet takes her work very seriously, often working long hours to perfect it. But she says she loves every minute of it. "I hadn't really thought about doing children's books, but once I did it I was hooked. I never looked back and I never wanted to do anything else after that."

H. Werner Zimmermann

SELECTED TITLES

 Illustrations only.

Born:
November 20, 1951, in Wörgl, Austria

Home:
Guelph, Ontario

Werner Zimmermann recalls being a poor reader when he was a kid, and he admits that for years this caused him to stay away from books. He also remembers not having many places to play in the town where he grew up, and finally turning to books as an escape. "I don't think I tweaked into books until grade six. It was a horrible, boring summer and I read these really neat adventure books by Enid Blyton. Here were kids on a sailboat who had real adventures — they had everything in the summer that I didn't."

Werner's introduction to making books was also a little unusual. It didn't come out of a discussion with a publisher, but rather from a discussion with a kindergarten teacher. "The first book I did was because my son was in kinder-

garten and he was having problems reading — he has the same difficulties with words that I do. We had him in French immersion and I went to the teacher asking for books that we could read to him. She pointed out that everything was written for kids who'd spent their first five years at home speaking French. So, I said: I'm an artist; is there something I could do?" That teacher seized the opportunity and asked Werner to do a Valentine's Day book about shapes. And so began the first draft of *A Circle Is Not a Valentine* and Werner Zimmermann's career in children's books.

Werner has a great respect for his young readers and prefers to create stories he knows they'll enjoy, rather than those with an obvious preachy moral. He is trying, perhaps, to reach kids who, like himself, aren't drawn to books right away. In fact, he confesses that he often gets so serious about his work that he becomes distracted and dips his paint brush in his coffee and drinks his paint water!

Werner is just as serious about sketching his subject matter, and he does this for days, long before he ever takes out his watercolours and pencil crayons. He recalls one sketching outing when, as he prepared his drawings for *Henny Penny*, Werner learned the difference between private chickens and public chickens. "Public chickens just act like chickens. Private chickens have a whole different kind of personality. I sat in a chicken coop and drew them there. The farmer looked at me as if I was nuts! It's neat collecting the little stuff to put into a book when you're really left alone to do it."

A PIG ON AN ESCALATOR

On another sketching outing, Werner recalls working on the pictures for *Farmer Joe Goes to the City*. "While drawing the scene on the escalators, I was asked to leave a prominent department store because they thought I was sketching the new and secret display being set up — as if I were a spy for the rivals. It was rather sad to leave, because the pig was having such a grand time on the escalator!

"I loved doing that book because I experience the same thing as Joe every time I need to shop for a gift. I am envious of him only because he got to take his animals. I can think of no greater fun than to take a cow, a pig and some chickens to a mall."

Werner welcomes feedback as he's working. "I've got a testing group right here: my kids and their friends. They're good. If they like it, they like it and if they don't like it, they tell me. I can be pretty protec-

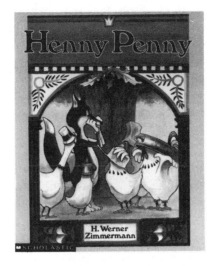

tive sometimes, too. They'll know when not to mention anything by the look on my face; they'll know I'm still working on it."

Werner is always striving to make his paintings better, although he admits to doubting he'll ever be completely satisfied with a project. "I admire those people who say: this is the way it was meant to be, and this is the way I've done it, and there it is — it's finished and it's done right."

For Werner, it isn't that cut and dried. He advises new illustrators not to expect the work to be easy, and to be willing to slug it out even when people are telling you it isn't worth the effort. "If you want to do it, then do it. Don't let people talk you out of it. Take good advice, but ignore the naysayers."

> *"When people ask me how I got into books I have to say: Face first."*

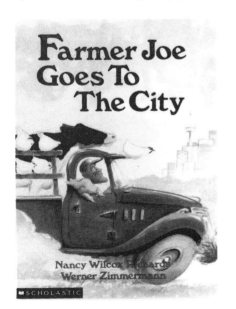

DO IT YOURSELF!

Werner Zimmermann says the secret to putting life into your drawings is to draw people and animals from the inside out. For this, stick figures are really valuable. He says they help an artist learn a lot about movement and suggests that you use them as your beginning point, adding features when you've established where your character will bend and how it will move.

Awards

As you go through this book, you will notice references to awards that many of the authors and illustrators have received. Many have received more awards than are listed here, including international awards, but there simply wasn't enough space to fit them all in.

Following is a brief description of each award mentioned in this book.

The Amelia Frances Howard-Gibbon Illustrator's Award
Awarded annually by the Canadian Library Association for the best illustrated children's book. The illustrator must be a Canadian citizen, and the book must be published in Canada on a Canadian subject.

The Canada Council Children's Literature Prize
In 1986 this award was renamed the Governor General's Award for Children's Literature. See description below.

Canadian Library Association Book of the Year Award for Children
Awarded annually at the Canadian Library Association's (CLA) annual conference by the Canadian Association for Children's Librarians to the author of the best Canadian children's book published that year.

Canadian Library Association Young Adult Book Award
Awarded annually by the CLA for the best work of creative literature (novel, play or poetry) for young adults. The author must be a Canadian citizen and the book must be published in Canada.

Elizabeth Mrazik-Cleaver Canadian Picture Book Award
Awarded annually, unless no book is judged deserving of the award, by the National Library of Canada and the International Board on Books for Young People to a Canadian children's book illustrator. Established in 1986 in memory of children's book illustrator Elizabeth Mrazik-Cleaver.

The Geoffrey Bilson Award for Historical Fiction for Young People
Awarded annually by The Canadian Children's Book Centre to a Canadian author of historical fiction for young people. Established in 1988 in memory of historian and children's author Geoffrey Bilson.

Governor General's Literary Awards
For Canadian citizens publishing books for young people, up to four prizes are awarded annually by the Canada Council in each of the following categories: text in an English language book, text in a French language book, illustrations in an English language book, illustrations in a French language book. Before 1987 this award was known as The Canada Council Children's Literature Prize.

IODE Violet Downey Book Award
Awarded annually by the National Chapter of the Canadian International Order of the Daughters of the Empire (IODE) for the best Canadian English language book published for children under fourteen years of age. This award may be divided between two people. Established in memory of Violet Downey, a benefactor of the National Chapter of the IODE.

Mr. Christie's™ Book Award
Six awards are presented annually by a panel of children's book specialists to the best Canadian children's books in each of the following categories: text in an English language book for children ages eight and under, text in an English language book for children ages nine to fourteen, text in a French language book for children ages eight and under, text in a French language book for children ages nine to fourteen, illustrations in an English language book, illustrations in a French language book. Sponsored by Christie Brown & Co., a division of Nabisco Brands Ltd.

Ruth Schwartz Children's Book Award
Awarded annually by the Canadian Booksellers Association and The Ontario Arts Council to a Canadian children's author. This award is voted on by a jury of children and may be divided between two people. Established in memory of Toronto Bookstore proprietor Ruth Schwartz.

Vicky Metcalf Award
Awarded annually by the Canadian Authors Association to a Canadian author who has published at least four books for children ages seven to seventeen.

Hosting an Author/Illustrator Visit

After introducing your students to the talented authors and illustrators interviewed in this book, you may want to go one step further and invite one or two to visit your school. Following are some tips for planning that visit.

Don't

Don't plan long sessions with each class. Unless your visitor has a special workshop prepared, forty-five minutes to an hour is about standard for a meet-the-author workshop.

Don't ask authors or illustrators to speak to more than thirty or forty students at a time, unless he has agreed in advance to address the entire student body. In fact, some may request even smaller groups, preferring intimate library readings and personal question-and-answer periods.

Don't expect your visitor to read or critique students' work unless she has agreed to do so in advance. This is a time-consuming task and one that detracts from the author's visit. Remember, you've invited this person to come and talk about her work, not to mark papers.

Don't leave the room while your visitor is giving his presentation. Authors and illustrators are not teachers and cannot be expected to control or discipline your students when you are out of the room.

Don't abandon your visitor in the staff room. Let everyone know that an author or illustrator is visiting the school and make sure that she gets a cup of coffee on arrival and meets the rest of the staff.

Don't saddle your visitor with thank-you letters and pictures from every student in the class. Authors and illustrators on school visits carry enough paper already, without having to be loaded down with hundreds of letters that they simply don't have time to read or answer.

Do

Plan your visit as early as possible. Many authors and illustrators accept only a few invitations a year, reserving the rest of their time for work.

Make sure that someone is available to take care of your visitor at all times, and be sure to introduce him or her to the school principal and to the teachers whose classes will be participating in the workshops. Also, be sure to point out the staff room, washrooms, library, telephone, etc.

Provide your visitor with a typed schedule of planned events in advance, indicating how long each session will be and when breaks are planned.

Tell your visitor about special writing programs or other meet-the-author visits you've had at your school to help him prepare for your visit. Students who have met with and spoken to several authors will be a very different audience from those who have never explored the writing process in a workshop environment.

Be sure to have available any chart paper, dictionaries, projectors and tables that your visitor might need. At the very least, remind students to bring sharpened pencils and plenty of paper to the workshop. The more prepared students are, the more time can be devoted to working with the author or illustrator.

Try to have the workshop location available and empty at least fifteen minutes before the session begins. This will allow your presenter time to set things up for the workshops and collect her thoughts.

Make sure that you and your students have read at least one of the visiting author's books. It's also a good idea to prepare for the question and answer period in advance to avoid running out of meaningful questions. (How often have visiting authors and illustrators been confronted with the terrible three: How old are you? Where do you get your ideas? and How much money do you make?)

Have on display as many of your visitor's books as possible and provide students with the opportunity to browse through them before the author or illustrator arrives.

Be sure to pay attention while your visitor is giving his presentation. Although it may be tempting to mark those last few papers while you have the chance, guest speakers need your attention as much as that of your students. Otherwise, how will you be able to comment on their presentation during the break?

Give your visitor one thank-you note. He or she will have time to read and enjoy it and have space in the car to take it home. Or better yet, why not send a birthday card later in the year reminding that person how much you enjoyed their visit? We've listed the birthdays of the authors and illustrators included in this book on page 113, but you might even want to add them to your class calendar.

What to do if you can't get an author or illustrator to visit

Professional writers and illustrators don't just work for children's publishers. Try inviting newspaper or magazine authors, illustrators, book designers and editors to visit your school and talk about their work. Even if you have lined up a children's author it may still be worthwhile to invite one of these people to show students how different types of publications are produced.

You may also be able to make special arrangements to correspond on paper or through the magic of video with your favourite author or illustrator. This, of course, would really depend on the author or illustrator and would require a fair bit of planning at your end. Try to let the students do as much of the work as possible and do whatever you can to make things easy for your "writer in correspondence."

Students may also be fascinated to meet some of the people who work in a publishing house (editors, art directors, marketing representatives). You could also arrange for them to tour a printing press or book bindery, to see how the books are actually made, after they have been written and edited.

Need help?

The Canadian Children's Book Centre has an extensive library of Canadian children's books, author/illustrator biographies and resource materials. They also sell author kits and publishing information packs for classrooms. Contact the centre for more information at:

> The Canadian Children's Book Centre
> 35 Spadina Rd.
> Toronto, Ontario M5R 2S9
> (416) 975-0010

The Storytellers' School of Toronto offers courses for budding storytellers; these are particularly helpful for librarians and teachers who enjoy reading aloud. Professional storytellers are also available for classroom visits. Call (416) 924-8625 for more information.

A call to the Writers' Union at (416) 868-6914 is one of the best ways to book an author visit for your school, or call individual publishers to line up your meet-the-author workshop.

Birthdays

January 1	Philippe Béha		August 5	Linda Hendry
January 2	Jean Little		August 12	Christiane Duchesne
January 12	Kim LaFave		August 28	Ted Harrison
January 14	Cora Taylor		August 31	Dennis Lee
February 3	Warabé Aska		September 1	Barbara Smucker
February 10	Brenda Clark		September 12	Kevin Major
February 18	Laszlo Gal		September 25	Eugenie Fernandes
February 22	Paul Kropp		October 20	Jo Ellen Bogart
March 29	Margaret Buffie		October 23	Gordon Korman
March 29	Ted Staunton		October 30	Robin Muller
March 31	Ian Wallace		November 3	Monica Hughes
April 4	Phoebe Gilman		November 3	Bernice Thurman Hunter
April 17	Martyn Godfrey		November 6	Robert Munsch
April 27	Michael Arvaarluk Kusugak		November 14	Carol Matas
April 30	Kit Pearson		November 16	Barbara Reid
May 4	Lyn Cook		November 20	Janet Wilson
May 26	Ron Broda		November 20	H. Werner Zimmermann
May 29	Michèle Lemieux		November 24	Eric Wilson
June 4	Maryann Kovalski		November 28	Sylvie Daigneault
June 17	Marie-Louise Gay		November 29	Eric Beddows
June 26	Michael Bedard		November 30	L. M. Montgomery
July 18	Gilles Tibo		December 6	Stéphane Poulin
July 20	Paulette Bourgeois		December 21	Claire Mackay
July 24	Gordon Penrose		December 28	Janet Lunn
August 1	Michael Martchenko			

On Becoming a Better Writer

When we asked the authors featured in this book how students could become better writers, every one of them said read, read, read. We also asked what their favourite books were when they were kids, and some books came up several times. These included:

The 500 Hats of Bartholomew Cubbins by Dr. Seuss.
The Alpine Path by L. M. Montgomery.
Anne of Green Gables by L. M. Montgomery.
Angus Is Lost by Marjorie Flack.
The Babar books by Jean de Brunhoff.
The Borrowers by Mary Norton.
Charlotte's Web by E. B. White.
Farmer Boy by Laura Ingalls Wilder.
Girl of the Limberlost by Gene Stratton-Porter.
The Great Brain series by John D. Fitzgerald.
The Hardy Boys series by Franklin W. Dixon.
Homer Price by Robert McCloskey.
Little House on the Prairie by Laura Ingalls Wilder.
Little Women by Louisa May Alcott.
The Nancy Drew series by Carolyn Keene.
The Ramona books by Beverly Cleary.
The Secret Garden by Frances Hodgson Burnett.
Stuart Little by E. B. White.
A Tree Grows in Brooklyn by Betty Smith.
The Wind in the Willows by Kenneth Grahame.
The Wizard of Oz by Frank L. Baum.
Comic books, and,
"Anything I could get my hands on!"

The writers also agreed on something else: they said write, write, write. The act of writing itself helps make you a better writer. Here are some idea starters for writing projects in your classroom:

The first rule of writing is to write about what you know. If you're the star player on the basketball team, write about that; if after school you help out with the family business, write about that. You'll find that because you're a kind of an expert on the subject, you'll never run out of ideas. You could also write about something very personal, like your best moment ever.

When you just can't think of anything to write about, work with a partner and write each other a few great opening lines. Try not to include too much information in these sentences. The idea is to jumpstart your imagination, not block it with all kinds of facts that will have to be worked in later. Try something like "Twenty minutes into his detention, Bob heard something moving inside his desk." or "As soon as she saw the worms, she knew she was in trouble."

Another way of coming up with ideas is to make a list of "what if"s. What if we were snowed in and couldn't leave the school for a week? What if I stopped chewing on pencils and started eating them instead?

After you've come up with at least twenty of these — the wilder, the better — pick your favourite and begin writing.

In a group, create a word-at-a-time story. (You'll need at least five people and a large piece of chart paper to do this one.) Begin by writing the words "once upon a time" at the top of the page, then each person in turn must add one word to the story. Continue taking turns until the story is finished.

A variation on the word-at-a-time story is a page-at-a-time story in which each person writes an entire page of the story before passing it on to the next person.

Try writing a favourite story from a different point of view. For instance, write the story of Snow White from the dwarves' point of view. Be careful to include only information than your new storyteller would know. You could also try writing a different ending for a favourite picture book or novel.

Draw a shape on a piece of paper, then on a separate sheet explain exactly how you drew it so someone else will be able to draw the same thing without looking at your picture. Then see how well your description worked. Is your writing precise?

Stretch your imagination by writing a tall tale to answer a simple question, such as Where did you get those shoes? or How long have you been waiting for the bus?

Mystery writers spend a great deal of time plotting out every detail of their stories. Plan the perfect crime for a mystery story of your own. (Remember, it's easiest if you write about what you know!)

Write a letter to the editor of a local newspaper or magazine. Or start your own school newsletter for kids who like the same things you do. For example, if you like sports your newsletter could include game scores, your own thoughts on how certain teams are doing, and information on upcoming sports events in your school and in your town or city.

Conduct your own interview with someone who interests you. You might want to read the book *Tell Me About Yourself: How to Interview Anyone from Your Friends to Famous People* to get some ideas about conducting an interview before you begin.

How good is your memory? Write a page or two describing everything you saw on your way to school today. Try to use as much detail as possible.

At one time, practically every school had a school song that described just what made their school special. Write a song about your school or class.

Write and illustrate your own picture book, then share it with a group of younger students in your school.

Rudyard Kipling's *Just So Stories* and the fables and legends of many aboriginal peoples provide explanations of how to the world came to be the way it is. Read some of these stories yourself, then write your own story to explain how the camel got his hump or why it snows in winter.

Suppose you were to become an author in ten years. Write a page about yourself for our 2004 edition of *Meet the Authors and Illustrators*.

Your Classroom Publishing Centre

Following are some great books to help get your gang going on their own publishing projects.

The CANSCAIP Companion. Copyright © 1991 by CANSCAIP Ltd. Pembroke Publishers, 1991.

Fine Print: A Story about Johann Gutenberg. Copyright © 1991 by J. Johansen Burch. Published by Carolrhoda Books.

A Guide to Classroom Publishing. Copyright © 1986 by Paulette Whitman and Jane Baskwill. Published by Scholastic Canada Ltd.

Hot off the Press. Copyright © 1991 by Ruth Crisman. Published by Lerner Publications Co.

How a Book Is Made. Copyright © 1986 by Aliki. Published by Thomas Y. Crowell.

How a Book Is Made. Copyright © 1989 by Friesen Printers.

How Newspapers Are Made. Copyright © 1989 by Sarah Walters. Published by Facts on File.

How to Capture Live Authors and Bring Them to Your Schools: Practical and Innovative Ways to Schedule Authors for Author in Residence Programs, Children's Literature Festivals and Young Authors' Days. Copyright © 1986 by David Melton. Published by Landmark Editions.

Meet the Authors and Illustrators. Copyright © 1991 by Deborah Kovacs and James Preller. Published by Scholastic Inc.

Meet the Authors and Illustrators: Volume Two. Copyright © 1993 by Deborah Kovacs and James Preller. Published by Scholastic Inc.

Newbery and Caldecott Medal Books. Copyright © 1986 by Lee Kingman. Published by Horn Books.

Presenting Children's Authors, Illustrators and Performers. Copyright © 1990 by Barbara Greenwood. Published by Pembroke Publishers Ltd.

Tell Me About Yourself: How to Interview Anyone from Your Friends to Famous People. Copyright © 1985 by D.L. Mabery. Published by Lerner Publications Co.

Write Every Day. Copyright © 1990 by Rosemary Alexander. Published by Scholastic Inc.

Write Now! Copyright © 1988 by Karleen Bradford. Published by Scholastic Canada Ltd.

Writing. Copyright © 1992 by Amanda Lewis. Published by Kids Can Press Ltd.

Writing Picture Books. Copyright © 1991 by Kathy Stinson. Published by Pembroke Publishers Ltd.

Additional Resource Materials

Eric Beddows

Granfield, Linda. "The Art of the Children's Book Illustrator." *Quill & Quire*, October 1985.

Oppel, Kenneth. "Ken Nutt (a.k.a. Eric Beddows): Zooming to the Top." *Quill & Quire*, August 1989.

Philippe Béha

Goedhart, Bernie. "Philippe Béha." *Quill & Quire*, October 1985.

Paulette Bourgeois

The Canadian Children's Book Centre. "Meet the Author: Paulette Bourgeois." *Children's Book News*, April 1987.

Margaret Buffie

The Canadian Children's Book Centre. "Meet the Author: Margaret Buffie." *Children's Book News*, Fall 1988.

Carver, Peter. "Margaret Buffie's Spirit Circle." *Quill & Quire*, November 1989.

Ross, Catherine Sheldrick. "An Interview with Paulette Bourgeois." *Canadian Children's Literature*, No. 49, 1988.

Telgen, Diane, ed. "Buffie, Margaret 1945–." *Something About the Author*. Gale Research Company, 1993. Vol. 71.

Lyn Cook

Kinsman, Claire D. "Waddell, Evelyn Margaret (Lyn Cook)." *Contemporary Authors*, Gale Research Company, 1975.

Mayden, Ruth. "Cook, Lyn." *Profiles*, The Canadian Library Association, 1975.

Commire, Anne, ed. "Waddell, Evelyn Margaret 1918– (Lyn Cook)." *Something About the Author*. Gale Research Company, 1976. Vol. 10.

Marie-Louise Gay

Davis, Marie. "Un penchant pour la diagonale: An Interview with Marie-Louise Gay." *Canadian Children's Literature*, No. 60, 1990.

Greenwood, Barbara. "Moonbeam on a Cat's Ear and Rainy Day Magic: Questions and Answers with Marie-Louise Gay." *CANSCAIP News*, Winter 1986.

O'Brian, Leacy. "An Interview with Marie-Louise Gay." *Canadian Materials*, March 1989.

Olendorf, Donna, ed. "Gay, Marie-Louise 1952–." *Something About the Author*. Gale Research Company, 1992. Vol. 68.

Phoebe Gilman

Commire, Anne, ed. "Gilman, Phoebe 1940–." *Something About the Author*. Gale Research Company, 1990. Vol. 58.

Gaitskell, Susan. "Introducing Phoebe Gilman." *CANSCAIP News*, Spring 1986.

O'Reilly, Gillian. "Phoebe Gilman: Winner of the 1993 Ruth Schwartz Award." *Canadian Bookseller*, June/July 1993.

Martyn Godfrey

The Canadian Children's Book Centre. "Meet the Author: Martyn Godfrey." *Children's Book News*, December 1986.

Godfrey, Martyn. "A Book Week Journal: My Visit to the Rock." *Quill & Quire*, February 1989.

Jenkinson, Dave. "Portraits." *Emergency Librarian*, September/October 1985.

McGoogan, Kenneth. "Godfrey's Odyssey: From Teaching to the Stars." *Quill & Quire*, 1986.

Bernice Thurman Hunter

The Canadian Children's Book Centre. "Meet the Author: Bernice Thurman Hunter." *Children's Book News*, December 1983.

Commire, Anne, ed. "Hunter, Bernice Thurman 1922–." *Something About the Author*. Gale Research Company, 1986. Vol. 45.

Evasuk, Stasia. "Age of Reason." *Toronto Star*, September 9, 1982.

Greenwood, Barbara. "Introducing Bernice Thurman Hunter." *CANSCAIP News*, Spring 1989.

Landsberg, Michele. "Book Takes Magic Look at Toronto's Depression Era." *Toronto Star*, October 15, 1981.

Wilkins, Charles. "Bernice Thurman Hunter: A World of Wonder from her Own Past." *Quill & Quire*, October 1987.

Monica Hughes

Commire, Anne, ed. "Hughes, Monica 1925–." *Something About the Author*. Gale Research Company, 1979. Vol. 15.

Greenwood, Barbara. "Introducing Monica Hughes." *CANSCAIP News*, Spring 1984.

Hughes, Monica. "The Writer's Quest." *Canadian Children's Literature*, No. 26, 1989.

Jones, Raymond E. "The Technological Pastoralist: A Conversation with Monica Hughes." *Canadian Children's Literature*, No. 44, 1988.

Malconnsen, Joan. "Writing Classics for Canadian Kids: Monica Hughes." *Quill & Quire*, February 1980.

Nakamura, Joyce, ed. "Monica Hughes 1925–." *Something About the Author Autobiography Series*. Gale Research Company, 1991. Vol. 11.

O'Reilly, Gillian. "Monica Hughes." *Jam Magazine*, June 1984.

Olendorf, Donna and Diane Telgen, ed. "Hughes, Monica (Ince) 1925–." *Something About the Author*. Gale Research Company, 1993. Vol. 70.

Wishinsky, Frieda. "Monica Hughes: Master of Myth." *Quill & Quire*, December 1989.

Dayal Kaur Khalsa

Commire, Anne, ed. "Khalsa, Dayal Kaur 1943–1989." *Something About the Author*. Gale Research Company, 1990. Vol. 62.

Cutler, May. "Dayal Kaur Khalsa 1943–1989: A Publisher's Tribute." *Canadian Materials*, November 1989.

"Dayal Kaur Khalsa—Her Secret Laughter." Tundra Fall 1993 Catalogue.

Granfield, Linda. "Dayal Kaur Khalsa 1943–1989." *Books in Canada*, November 1989.

Lyons, Terri L. "Dayal Kaur Khalsa." *Canadian Children's Literature*, No. 59, 1990.

Gordon Korman

Commire, Anne, ed. "Korman, Gordon 1963–." *Something About the Author*. Gale Research Company, 1987. Vol. 49.

Ferns, Chris. "An Interview with Gordon Korman." *Canadian Children's Literature*, No. 38, 1985.

Morgan, Joanna. "Kid Lit." *Today Magazine*, June 6, 1981.

Maryann Kovalski

Bildfell, Laurie. "The Art of the Children's Book Illustrator." *Quill & Quire*, October 1985.

Commire, Anne, ed. "Kovalski, Maryann 1951–." *Something About the Author*. Gale Research Company, 1990. Vol. 58.

Wagner, Dale. "Introducing Maryann Kovalski." *CANSCAIP News*, Summer 1989.

Paul Kropp

Commire, Ann, ed. "Kropp, Paul (Stephan) 1948–." *Something About the Author*. Gale Research Company, 1984. Vol. 38.

Hancock, Pat. "Introducing Paul Kropp." *CANSCAIP News*, Spring 1993.

Vanderhoof, Ann. "Hot Topics for Cool Readers." *Quill & Quire*, January 1980.

Dennis Lee

Commire, Anne, ed. "Lee, Dennis (Beynon) 1939–." *Something About the Author*. Gale Research Company, 1978. Vol. 14.

Lee, Dennis. "Roots and Play: Writing as a 35-Year-Old Children." *Canadian Children's Literature*, No. 4, 1976.

Ross, Catherine and Cory Bieman Davies. "Re-realizing Mother Goose: An Interview with Dennis Lee on Jelly Belly." *Canadian Children's Literature*, No. 33, 1984.

Jean Little

"An Interview with Jean Little." *Grail: An Ecumenical Journal*, December 1989.

Olendorf, Donna, ed. "Little, Jean 1932–." *Something About the Author*. Gale Research Company, 1992. Vol. 68.

Frazer, Frances. "Something on Jean Little." *Canadian Children's Literature*, No. 53, 1989.

Little, Jean. *Little by Little: A Writer's Education*. Penguin Books Canada Ltd., 1987.

Little, Jean. *Stars Come Out Within*. Penguin Books Canada Ltd., 1990.

Nakamura, Joyce, ed. "Jean Little 1932–." *Something About the Author Autobiography Series*. Gale Research Company, 1989. Vol. 17.

Ross, Catherine. "An Interview with Jean Little." *Canadian Children's Literature*, No. 34, 1984.

Janet Lunn

Barkhouse, Joyce. "Introducing Janet Lunn." *CANSCAIP News*, Spring 1985.

Nakamura, Joyce, ed. "Janet Lunn 1928–." *Something About the Author Autobiography Series*. Gale Research Company, 1991. Vol. 12.

Olendorf, Donna, ed. "Lunn, Janet 1928–." *Something About the Author*. Gale Research Company, 1992. Vol. 68.

Claire Mackay

Commire, Anne, ed. "Mackay, Claire 1930–." *Something About the Author*. Gale Research Company, 1985. Vol. 40.

Mackay, Claire. "Real Plums in Imaginary Cakes." *Canadian Children's Literature*, No. 54, 1989.

Kevin Major

Commire, Ann, ed. "Major, Kevin 1949–." *Something About the Author*. Gale Research Company, 1983. Vol. 32.

"Kevin Major 1949–" *Children's Literature Review*, Vol. 11

Posesorski, Sherie. "Kevin Major." *Books in Canada*, December 1984.

"Tales of Newfoundland Youth Spell Success for Kevin Major." *Atlantic Insight*, November 1984.

Michael Martchenko

Commire, Anne, ed. "Marchenko, Michael 1942–." *Something About the Author*. Gale Research Company, 1988. Vol. 50.

Vanderhoof, Ann. "The Art of the Children's Book Illustrator." *Quill & Quire*, October 1985.

L.M. Montgomery

Gillen, Mollie. *Lucy Maud Montgomery*. Fitzhenry & Whiteside Ltd., 1978.

"L (ucy) M (aud) Montgomery 1974–1942." *Children's Literature Review*, Vol. 8.

Montgomery, L. M. *The Alpine Path*. Fitzhenry & Whiteside Ltd., 1917.

Robin Muller

The Canadian Children's Book Centre. "Meet the Author: Robin Muller." *Children's Book News*, March 1985.

Greenwood, Barbara. "Introducing Robin Muller." *CANSCAIP News*, Spring 1990.

Robert Munsch

The Canadian Children's Book Centre. "Meet the Author: Robert Munsch." *Book Times*, September 1981.

Collins, Janet. "Giant Problem or What Is a Kid's Book Anyway?" *Canadian Materials*, May 1990.

Commire, Anne, ed. "Munsch, Robert N. 1945–." *Something About the Author*. Gale Research Company, 1988. Vol. 50.

Crawford, C. Lee. "Happy Anniversary, Bob!" *Quill & Quire*, April 1989.

Kondo, David. "Robert Munsch: An Interview." *Canadian Children's Literature*, No. 43, 1986.

Kit Pearson

Schwartz, Ellen. "Introducing Kit Pearson." *CANSCAIP News*, Summer 1990.

Gordon Penrose

Olendorf, Donna, ed. "Penrose, Gordon 1925– (Dr. Zed)." *Something About the Author*. Gale Research Company, 1991. Vol. 66.

Rhval, Michael. "Turning Kids on to Science: Dr. Zed, I Presume?" *Quill & Quire*, February 1982.

Stéphane Poulin

Goedhart, Bernie. "Stéphane Poulin's Sensitive Approach to Life and Art." *Quill & Quire*, August 1987.

Barbara Reid

The Canadian Children's Book Centre. "Meet the Illustrator: Barbara Reid." *Children's Book News*, September 1985.

Graitskell, Susan. "An Interview with Barbara Reid." *Canadian Children's Literature*, No. 56, 1989.

McDougall, Carol. "Introducing Barbara Reid." *CANSCAIP Book News*, Spring 1988.

Barbara Smucker

"Barbara (Claassen) Smucker 1915–" *Children's Literature Review*, Vol. 10.

The Canadian Children's Book Centre. "Meet the Author: Barbara Smucker." *Book Times*, 1980.

Davies, Cory Bieman. "An Interview with Barbara Smucker." *Canadian Children's Literature*, No. 22, 1981.

Nakamura, Joyce, ed. "Barbara (Claassen) Smucker 1915–." *Something About the Author Autobiography Series.* Gale Research Company, 1991. Vol. 11.

Salata, Estelle. "Barbara Smucker." *CANSCAIP News*, Fall 1990.

Ted Staunton

The Canadian Children's Book Centre. "Meet the Author: Ted Staunton." *Children's Book News*, June 1985.

Ian Wallace

The Canadian Children's Book Centre. "Meet the Author: Ian Wallace." *Children's Book News*, June 1984.

Commire, Anne, ed. "Wallace, Ian 1950–." *Something About the Author.* Gale Research Company, 1989. Vol. 56.

Wallace, Ian. "When Fort Nelson's Kids Won Ian Wallace." *Quill & Quire*, February 1985.

Eric Wilson

Commire, Ann, ed. "Wilson, Eric H. 1940–." *Something About the Author.* Gale Research Company, 1984. Vol. 34.

Eric Wilson's Canada. (video) Magic Lantern Communications, 1991.

Jenkinson, Dave. "Eric Wilson." Profiles 2, *The Canadian Library Association*, 1982.

Locher, Frances C., ed. "Wilson, Eric H." *Contemporary Authors*, Gale Research Company, 1981.

Meet the Author: Eric Wilson. (film strip and video) School Services of Canada, 1987.

Senn, Roma. "Whodunit? Eric Wilson." *Atlantic Insight*, October 1981.

H. Werner Zimmermann

Maruszeczka, Greg. "Being There." *Canadian Materials*, September 1993.

O'Brien, Leacy. "Watermelon Blue." *Canadian Materials*, May 1990.

Acknowledgements

I would like to extend a special thank you to all of the authors and illustrators who took time from their busy schedules to answer my questions. It was a real treat getting a glimpse behind the scenes!

Thanks, too, to my editor, Diane Kerner, who offered suggestions when they were needed most and to all the publishers who made this edition of *Meet the Authors and Illustrators* possible. Additional thanks go to the following editors, publicists and agents: Maral Bablanian, Janine Belzak, Kirsten Cook, Virginia Evans, Harriot Heller, Eric Johnston, Jeffrey Kay, Joanne Kellock, Ginette Kong, Bernice Korman, Caroline Krinsley, Alison Lester, Peter London, Kathy Lowinger, Michel Luppens, Jo McNeill, Catherine Mitchell, Joan Puterbough, Tracy Read, Jane Roland, Dara Rowland, Ann Schone, Scott Sellers, Carmel Shaffer, Patricia Silk, Sally Tindal, Chantale Vaillancourt, Jane Weeks and Rhea Wilmshurst.

Excerpts included in the Dayal Kaur Khalsa piece came from the November 1987 issue of *The Tundra Newsletter* and from the Canadian Children's Book Centre's biography. Permission to excerpt obtained from the publisher, Tundra Books, and from The Canadian Children's Book Centre, respectively.

Excerpt included in the Barbara Smucker piece came from Fall 1990 issue of *CANSCAIP News* by Estelle Salata. Permission to excerpt obtained from the author.

Resources used in the writing of this book

The Canadian Children's Book Centre. *Introducing Canadian Children's Authors and Illustrators.*

The Children's Book Council. *Children's Books Awards and Prizes.* The Children's Book Council Inc., 1992.

Greenwood, Barbara, ed. *The CANSCAIP Companion.* CANSCAIP, 1991.

Montgomery, L. M. *The Alpine Path.* Fitzhenry & Whiteside Ltd., 1917.

Photography Credits

Author/illustrator photographs

Michael Bedard © Merrilee Brand; Ron Broda courtesy of Scholastic Canada Ltd.; Margaret Buffie © Towne Studios Ltd.; Brenda Clark courtesy of Kids Can Press Ltd.; Sylvie Daigneault courtesy of Scholastic Canada Ltd.; Christiane Duchesne © André Panneton; Eugenie Fernandes courtesy of Scholastic Canada Ltd.; Laszlo Gal © Raffaella Gal; Martyn Godfrey courtesy of Scholastic Canada Ltd.; Monica Hughes © R. Hughes; Bernice Thurman Hunter courtesy of Scholastic Canada Ltd.; Dayal Kaur Khalsa courtesy of Tundra Books Inc.; Gordon Korman courtesy of Scholastic Canada Ltd.; Maryann Kovalski courtesy of Scholastic Canada Ltd.; Michael Kusugak © Paul Heersink; Dennis Lee © Susan Perly; Jean Little courtesy of Penguin Books Canada Ltd.; Janet Lunn courtesy of Lester Publishing Ltd.; Claire Mackay courtesy of Scholastic Canada Ltd.; Kevin Major © Ned Pratt; Carol Matas courtesy of Scholastic Canada Ltd.; Lucy Maud Montgomery courtesy of The Canadian Children's Book Centre; Robin Muller courtesy of Scholastic Canada Ltd.; Kit Pearson © Russell Kelly; Barbara Reid © Ian Crysler; Ted Staunton courtesy of Kids Can Press Ltd.; Cora Taylor courtesy of Scholastic Canada Ltd.; Eric Wilson © Lawrence McLagan; Janet Wilson © John Reeves; H. Werner Zimmermann courtesy of Scholastic Canada Ltd.

Book covers

Warabé Aska
Aska's Animals © 1991 by David Day. Illustrations © 1991 by Warabé Aska. Reprinted by permission of Doubleday Canada Ltd. *Seasons* © 1990 by Warabé Aska. Reprinted by permission of Doubleday Canada Ltd.

Michael Bedard
Emily © 1992 by Michael Bedard. Illustrations © 1992 by Barbara Cooney. Reprinted by permission of Lester Publishing Ltd. *Redwork* © 1992 by Michael Bedard. Reprinted by permission of Lester Publishing Ltd.

Eric Beddows
Who Shrank My Grandmother's House? © 1992 by Barbara Esbensen. Illustrations © 1992 by Eric Beddows. Reprinted by permission of Douglas & McIntyre. *Zoom Upstream* © 1992 by Tim Wynne-Jones. Illustrations © 1992 by Eric Beddows. Reprinted by permission of Douglas & McIntyre.

Philippe Béha
What Do the Fairies Do With All Those Teeth? © 1989 by Michel Luppens. Illustrations © 1989 by Philippe Béha. Reprinted by permission of Scholastic Canada Ltd.

Jo Ellen Bogart
Gifts © 1994 by Jo Ellen Bogart. Illustrations © 1994 by Barbara Reid. Reprinted by permission of Scholastic Canada Ltd. *Two Too Many* © 1994 by Jo Ellen Bogart. Illustrations © 1994 by Yvonne Cathcart. Reprinted by permission of Scholastic Canada Ltd.

Paulette Bourgeois
Franklin Is Bossy © 1993 by Paulette Bourgeois. Illustrations © 1993 by Brenda Clark. Reprinted by permission of Kids Can Press Ltd. *The Amazing Potato Book* © 1991 by Paulette Bourgeois. Illustrations © 1991 by Linda Hendry. Reprinted by permission of Kids Can Press Ltd.

Ron Broda
The Little Crooked Christmas Tree © 1990 by Michael Cutting. Illustrations © 1990 by Ron Broda. Reprinted by permission of Scholastic Canada Ltd. *Waters* © 1993 by Edith Newlin Chase. Illustrations © 1993 by Ron Broda. Reprinted by permission of Scholastic Canada Ltd.

Margaret Buffie
My Mother's Ghost © 1992. Reprinted by permission of Kids Can Press Ltd. *Who Is Frances Rain?* © 1987. Reprinted by permission of Kids Can Press Ltd.

Brenda Clark
Franklin Is Bossy © 1993 by Paulette Bourgeois. Illustrations © 1993 by Brenda Clark. Reprinted by permission of Kids Can Press Ltd. *Little Fingerling* © 1989 by Monica Hughes. Illustrations © 1989 by Brenda Clark. Reprinted by permission of Kids Can Press Ltd.

Lyn Cook
The Bells on Finland Street © 1950, 1991. Reprinted by permission of Scholastic Canada Ltd.; *Samantha's Secret Room* © 1963. Reprinted by permission of Scholastic Canada Ltd.

Sylvie Daigneault
Mama's Bed © 1993 by Jo Ellen Bogart. Illustrations © 1993 by Sylvie Daigneault. Reprinted by permission of Scholastic Canada Ltd.; *Sarah Saw a Blue Macaw* © 1991 Jo Ellen Bogart. Illustrations © 1991 by Sylvie Daigneault. Reprinted by permission of Scholastic Canada Ltd.

Christiane Duchesne
La 42ᵉ soeur de Bébert © 1993 by Christiane Duchesne. Reprinted by permission of Éditions Québec/Amérique Inc. *Quel beau petit!* © 1984 by Barbara Reid. Text © 1986 by Christiane Duchesne. Reprinted by permission of Scholastic Canada Ltd.

Eugenie Fernandes
The Tree that Grew to the Moon © 1994 by Eugenie Fernandes. Reprinted by permission of Scholastic Canada Ltd. *Waves in the Bathtub* © 1993 by Eugenie Fernandes. Reprinted by permission of Scholastic Canada Ltd.

Allison Gertridge

This book is for my parents, who brought me Frederick stories and family fun night, and for Wally, who knows why.

Born:
December 11, 1967 in
Lindsay, Ontario
Home:
Richmond Hill, Ontario

Allison Gertridge credits her father with inspiring her to write. "Practically every night when I was growing up, he would make up an original story," she says, "and he *always* knew just how to help me rework my poems and stories — and he still does."

Allison performed with a children's theatre troupe and as a storyteller before spending four years as a children's book editor for Scholastic Canada. Today, she has her own company, Think Publishing, and works as a freelance writer and workshop coordinator.